The Williamsburg
COOKBOOK

The Williamsburg
COOKBOOK

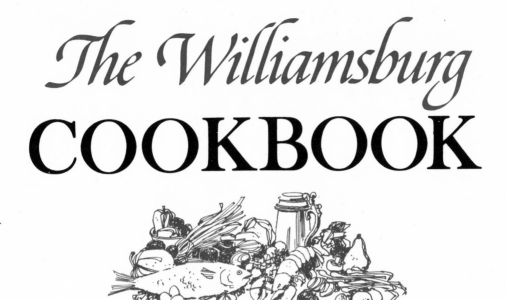

Traditional and Contemporary Recipes
Initially Compiled and Adapted by Letha Booth
and the Staff of Colonial Williamsburg

With Commentary by Joan Parry Dutton

Color Photographs by Taylor Biggs Lewis, Jr.
Line Drawings by Vernon Wooten

Published by
THE COLONIAL WILLIAMSBURG FOUNDATION
Williamsburg, Virginia

Distributed by
HOLT, RINEHART AND WINSTON
New York, New York

Distributed simultaneously in Canada by
Holt, Rinehart and Winston of Canada, Limited.
Updated and enlarged edition, 1975
Second printing, 1976
This book was designed by Vernon Wooten.

Library of Congress Cataloging in Publication Data

Booth, Letha, comp.
   The Williamsburg cookbook.

   Includes index.
   1. Cookery, American—Virginia.   I. Colonial Williamsburg Foundation.   II. Title
TX715.725 1975   641.5'9755   75-2328
ISBN 0-03-086704-5 (Holt, Rinehart & Winston) hardbd

   ISBN 0-910412-92-8 (Colonial Williamsburg) softbd

Cover:

A pot of hearty Brunswick Stew is in the making at Chowning's Tavern, complete with all the fresh vegetables and tender chicken that have made it a favorite with Virginians for centuries.

Frontispiece:

Chickens are golden-brown on the spit, in the Brush-Everard kitchen, and a baked Virginia Ham garnished with spiced fruits and water cress is ready for the dinner table. The cook puts a finishing touch on a cut of beef. In front of the vegetables, left to right, are a Sally Lunn, Apple Pie, Indian Corn Sticks and Muffins.

Contents

The Williamsburg
COOKBOOK

Part I

Building a Tradition

Building a Tradition

For well over three centuries Virginia has been famed for its good food and hospitality. By 1699, when Williamsburg was founded, Virginians were enjoying a bill of fare that was probably unrivaled. The Tidewater, with its forests and its waterways, was a primeval paradise of fish and game, just as England, an island surrounded by fish, was once a vast game preserve. Domestic animals, brought over from England, thrived in the new climate, and so did English vegetables and fruits. Then there were the Indians' crops, above all their corn. The first settlers had brought wheat with them, but soon they were growing more corn than wheat.

Engaged one way or another in tobacco growing, almost all Virginians lived on the land. Williamsburg was small but beautiful, as befitted the seat of government. With no more than two thousand permanent residents, for most of the year it enjoyed quiet and ease. But during Publick Times, when the courts convened in the spring and fall, when the Assembly met, on royal birthdays, and on other special occasions, the town grew almost overnight. Williamsburg became the setting for carnival and for affairs of law and state. It was vibrant with

1

color, dust, and noise, agog with all the robustness and all the elegance of Virginia's Golden Age.

To cope with such regular invasions, an extraordinary number of "convenient ordinaries or inns for accommodation of strangers" offered meals, drinks, and lodging. The taverns of Williamsburg, like the taverns of London in those days, played an integral part in town life. Their patrons were councilors and burgesses, ship captains and lawyers, merchants and planters, who met within their doors to transact business, talk politics, play cards, and gossip over a bottle of wine, a bowl of punch, or a tankard of ale.

The tavern-keeper was a man of consequence. He received his guests in the true manner of a host, discussed with them matters of moment, and judged when to keep his counsel and when to disclose it. Above all, each tavern-keeper was expected to provide his patrons with a bill of fare (a choice of fish, meat, fruits, and vegetables in season) and a choice of wines comparable to those served by planters at home. Only those taverns with good cooks in the kitchen survived.

Virginians, being mostly of English and Scottish stock, ate much the same kind of food as did Britons. English cookbooks were the Virginia housewife's standby. Two of the most popular eighteenth-century cookbooks used in Virginia were *The Art of Cookery Made Plain and Easy* by Mrs. Hannah Glasse and *The Compleat Housewife* by Mrs. E. Smith. First published in London in 1727, *The Compleat Housewife* was reprinted by William Parks of Williamsburg in 1742. It was the first cookbook published in British America.

A copy of William Parks's reprint belonging to the Virginia Historical Society was rebound by C. Clement Samford, Williamsburg's master bookbinder, 222 years after the book was first sold. Samford gave it a new brown calfskin cover and matching end sheets of old paper; the interior pages were in exceptionally good condition.

Bookbinding is but one of the traditional crafts still being carried on in Williamsburg. Others are to be seen in the many craft shops and outdoor demonstrations. The exhibition buildings and taverns in the Historic Area, like the town itself, are even busier now than they were in colonial days, for not only Virginians but presidents of the United States, foreign heads of state, and visitors from all walks of life and most parts of the world come to what was the capital of colonial Virginia.

Three eighteenth-century taverns, the King's Arms, Christiana Campbell's, and Josiah Chowning's, provide dining facilities for visitors.

2

(Colonial Williamsburg's entirely modern Williamsburg Inn, Williamsburg Lodge, the Motor House and the Cascades, just outside the limits of the Historic Area, provide both meals and lodging beyond any early traveler's imagination.) In each of the taverns, the chairs, tables, and tableware reflect colonial styles in furnishings. The people who welcome and wait on visitors in the candlelit dining rooms wear colonial dress. The amenities that restaurateurs require—the modern cookstoves, refrigerators, and cooking utensils—are all behind the scenes.

Menus, printed in old-style Caslon, a type face much used in America in colonial times, list modern dishes along with the old familiar southern foods: chowders, fried chicken, spoon bread and corn sticks, pecan pie, and the Tidewater's specialities of Virginia ham and Sally Lunn.

Many of the recipes in this book are derived from those that our great-great-grandmothers used; others are in the tradition of southern cooking; and some blend the tastes of the old and new worlds. Although she is of the twentieth century, Mrs. Letha Booth is part of the Williamsburg tradition. She was the manager of Travis House, Colonial Williamsburg's first restaurant in the eighteenth-century manner, from 1946 until 1951, and thereafter until her retirement she managed the famous King's Arms Tavern. Most of the recipes in this book were initially compiled and adapted for the home kitchen by Mrs. Booth. Others have been added and similarly adapted by more recent members of the Colonial Williamsburg restaurant operations staff. All were written and retested by Mrs. Grace Sumner, Norfolk food editor.

Selected Menus for Various
and Special Occasions

Meals Fit for a King— or a Queen

M any foreign heads of state invited by the president of the United States for an official visit to this country come to Williamsburg. The visit gives them a chance to see something of what colonial America was like and to spend a quiet evening following the long flights from their homeland before being whisked off by helicopter the next morning and set down on the White House lawn.

On the last lap of a three-week tour of the eastern United States in 1957, Queen Elizabeth and Prince Philip came to Williamsburg, at the invitation of Governor Thomas B. Stanley of Virginia, to attend the 350th anniversary celebration of the founding of Jamestown. Colonial Williamsburg's dinner in their honor was most carefully planned. By discreet inquiries their hosts in Williamsburg learned the royal couple's eating preferences, as noted along their route, and the menu that was to be presented to them in Washington the day before, as well as that in New York City the following day.

The dinner set before them, compared with the lavishness of colonial entertaining, was simple, but it did include some traditional dishes in modern dress. In her letter of thanks Queen Elizabeth wrote that she and Prince Philip had enjoyed that dinner more than any other dinner in their travels anywhere.

Dinner in honor of Her Majesty, Queen Elizabeth II and His Royal Highness, Prince Philip
Williamsburg Inn

Clear Green Turtle Soup, Amontillado*   *Cheese Straws*

Mushrooms Bordelaise
(Williams and Humbert Dry Sack)
Boneless Breast of Chicken* *with Virginia Ham**
Baby Green Beans, Amandine
(Bâtard Montrachet, 1953)
Avocado Slices   French Dressing

Fresh Strawberry Mousse*
(Veuve Clicquot Yellow Label, Dry)
Demitasse and Liqueurs

In colonial days it was customary for royal governors to celebrate British sovereigns' birthnights. On a May evening in 1976, the members of the British Bicentennial Heritage Mission were invited to a supper at the Governor's Palace to honor one of their number, the Earl of Dunmore, and to mark the first time a descendant of a royal governor of Virginia had dined at the Palace since Virginia became a commonwealth. The Earl's ancestor, the 4th Earl of Dunmore, was the last royal governor of Virginia. He fled the colony in 1775, ending 168 years of British rule.

The affair was much in the spirit of a party Governor and Lady Dunmore gave on the evening of January 18, 1775, the birthnight of Queen Charlotte.

WEDNESDAY last being the day for celebrating the birth of her Majesty, his Excellency the Earl of Dunmore gave a

7

* *Recipe is in this cookbook; see index for page number.*

ball and elegant entertainment at the Palace to a numerous company of Ladies and Gentlemen. The same day his Lordship's youngest daughter was baptised in the name VIRGINIA.

The supper was similar to those served in the governor's house in the eighteenth century. Governor Dunmore had large farm holdings that provided a wide variety of meats, fruits, and vegetables. The entertainment was colonial in style also. Musicians, singers, a conjurer, a juggler, and several acrobats added to the gaiety of the evening.

Supper given for the British Bicentennial Heritage Mission
in honor of the Earl of Dunmore
Governor's Palace

Cold Plantation Beef
(Château St. Paul, Haut-Médoc)

*Roast Virginia Quail, Peach Garnish**
*Sweet Potato Pudding**

Garden Salad Greens
Stilton Cheese

*Bicentennial Tart**
(Charles Heidsieck, Brut)
Demitasse and Cordials

* Recipe is in this cookbook; see index for page number.

When the clock strikes midnight at the ▶ Williamsburg Inn, champagne toasts will welcome in the new year. Around the party table, counter-clockwise, are Marinated Shrimp in Fresh Dill; Barbecued Baby Spareribs; Biscuits Spread with Virginia Ham Pâté; Cheddar Cheese and Olive Balls; Salted Peanuts; Skewered Pineapple and Strawberries in Kirsch; and Chilled Backfin Crabmeat with Mayonnaise.

Meals Fit for a King—or a Queen

Dinner in honor of
His Excellency Petrus J. S. de Jong
Prime Minister of the Netherlands
Carter's Grove Plantation

Hors d'Oeuvres
*Tiny Ham Biscuits**

*Fresh Backfin Crabmeat**
(mixed with Mayonnaise, Salt and Pepper)

Assorted Crackers

❧🙞

Dinner
Consommé with Swan Pâté

*Lamb Chops Alden**
Pennsylvania Stuffed Peppers
Noodle Casserole

Mixed Green Salad
Lemon and Olive Oil Dressing
Cheese Straws

Fresh Whole Strawberries
Granulated and Powdered Sugar
Sweet Cream and Sour Cream

Demitasse
Cordials

* *Recipe is in this cookbook; see index for page number.*

◄ *A simplified version of the Crown of the Turtle Feast at King's Arms Tavern makes a festive holiday dinner, with Veal Birds Garnished with Fresh Mushrooms and Artichoke Bottoms served as the main course. Also on the menu: Cream of Oyster and Spinach Soup; King's Arms Tavern Creamed Onions with Peanuts (in casserole at left) and Sweet Potatoes (right); Fresh Garden Salad, with Sally Lunn and Indian Corn Sticks; and Pecan Pie for dessert.*

Family Meals, Then and Now

By our standards, family meals in the old days were prodigious. Not necessarily for the quantity of food consumed, for many of the colony's leading men ate sparingly, but for the variety of dishes on hand.

Tidewater Virginians continued the English custom of a hearty breakfast, usually between nine and ten o'clock, of venison, game or poultry, and ham. A new item was the fresh-baked hot breads, often Indian cakes, in what came to be recognized as "the Virginia fashion." Dinner was from around half-past two to four. The choice of dishes was wide: beef, roast pig, mutton, fish, ham of course, greens, and a pudding and cheese to round it off. Supper was light and late, between nine and ten, of oysters, "battered" eggs, or bread and cheese, wine or cider, fruit, and some light dessert.

The dining table was indeed a groaning board, for families were larger in those days and Virginians kept open house to an extraordinary degree. Kith and kin arriving unexpectedly might stay for weeks at a time, and even a passing stranger was welcome.

Our way of living, and consequently our eating habits, are now vastly different. Today's family menus reflect the change.

*Chowning's Tavern Brunswick Stew**

Salad of Mixed Greens   *Manchet Bread**
*with Oil and Vinegar Dressing**

*Wine Jelly Mold with Custard Sauce**

❧

Virginia Ham and Brandied Peaches**

*Carrot Pudding**   *Green Beans*

*King's Arms Tavern Greengage Plum Ice Cream**

*Cinnamon Squares**

❧

*Ginger Beef**

*Rice or Grits Soufflé**   *Brussels Sprouts with Chestnuts**

*Lemon Chess Tarts**

❧

*Chesapeake Oyster Bisque**

*Williamsburg Inn Breast of Turkey Supreme**

Rice or Noodles   *Scalloped Tomatoes and Artichoke Hearts**

*Apple Pie**

11

* *Recipe is in this cookbook; see index for page number.*

Building a Tradition

*Baked Eggs in Casserole**
Frozen Fruit Salad with Williamsburg Lodge Honey Dressing**
*Williamsburg Lodge Orange Wine Cake**

❧❀❧

*Chilled King's Arms Tavern Cream of Peanut Soup**
*Christiana Campbell's Tavern Salmagundi**
*Sally Lunn**
*Raspberry Ice**   *Williamsburg Inn Pecan Bars**

❧❀❧

*Williamsburg Inn Chicken and Dumplings**
Green Peas with Whole Onions
Black Cherry Salad with French Dressing**
*Williamsburg Lodge Bavarian Cream**

❧❀❧

*Chowning's Tavern Sautéed Backfin Crabmeat**
*Christiana Campbell's Tavern Spoon Bread**
Buttered Fresh Asparagus
*Christiana Campbell's Tavern Tipsy Squire**

* *Recipe is in this cookbook; see index for page number.*

Family Meals, Then and Now

Essence of Tomato*
Cascades Baked Stuffed Flounder*
Cascades Ratatouille*
*Salad of Boston Lettuce with Williamsburg Inn
Regency Dressing**
Christiana Campbell's Tavern Rum Cream Pie*

⚜

Melon Balls with Virginia Ham*
Travis House Oysters*
Indian Corn Sticks*
Salad of Mixed Greens with Garlic French Dressing*
Black Forest Cake*

* *Recipe is in this cookbook; see index for page number.*

Christmas Feast and Festival

In Williamsburg not only Christmas itself but the Christmas Season— as it was called in colonial days—is observed. The season today runs from December 19 to January 6, known in the English calendar and observed for centuries as Twelfth Night.

True, the festivities of today are more elaborate than they were in colonial days. Then Christmas was primarily a religious festival. However, towards the end of the colonial period balls, foxhunts, and the firing of the Christmas guns were part and parcel of the holiday season, and there is evidence that plantation owners' wives concerned themselves and lent a hand in the making of what had become traditional holiday fare. Nor were friends in England forgotten. In August 1770, with forethought of the time it took a sailing ship to make the Atlantic crossing, Mrs. Martha Goosley and Mrs. Mary Ambler of Yorktown sent to John Norton, merchant of London, two Christmas turkeys and "hams to eat with them."

Today, Colonial Williamsburg keeps what most of us think of as the old-style Christmas. Old English customs, the yule-log ceremony and the wassail bowl, have been revived. Adapted from the German custom, a living evergreen serves proudly as a Christmas tree on Market Square. With a candle in every window and a wreath on every door, the Historic Area is aglow, and there is music in the air. Rich seasonal fare, a blend of traditional and relatively newly devised dishes, makes up the taverns' and the restaurants' twelve-days groaning boards.

The Crown of the Turtle is the big showpiece gourmets take delight in during Christmas week. The forerunner of the eighteenth-century dish was boar's head, which was the festive Christmas dish in medieval England. For those dining out at the castle, the head was armed with tusks and decorated elaborately. The homely version was peasant fare: a somewhat highly spiced and glazed piece of cold boiled bacon.

Mrs. Raffald, author of *The Experienced English House-Keeper . . .*, first published in 1769, used the phrase "the crown of the turtle" for an elaborate arrangement of a calf's head dressed as a mock turtle and served on a turtle shell. The "crown" was a ball of forcemeat placed between the calf's ears.

Colonial Williamsburg has interpreted this feast by serving a calf's head wearing a forcemeat crown and garnished with sweetbreads, artichoke bottoms, veal birds, mushrooms, and truffles—the whole being presented on a silver tray instead of a turtle shell.

Christmas Day

*Wassail**   *Cheese Wafers**

*Williamsburg Inn Chilled Crab Gumbo**

Roast Young Tom Turkey

Fresh Mushroom Dressing

King's Arms Tavern   *Heart of Lettuce,*
*Creamed Celery with Pecans**   *Cascades Pepper Dressing**

*Eggnog Pie**

and/or

*Ambrosia**   *Mince Pie with Rum Butter Sauce**

* *Recipe is in this cookbook; see index for page number.*

Building a Tradition

The Crown of the Turtle Feast

In the eighteenth century veal birds were used as garnishes for many elaborate concoctions. This menu calls for them to be served as the main course. With its own garnishes of artichokes and fresh mushrooms this dish is an appropriate substitute for the feast in its entirety.

FIRST COURSE

Soup Remove	*Cream of Oyster and Spinach Soup**
Meat	*Veal Birds Garnished with Fresh Mushrooms and Artichoke Bottoms**
Vegetables	*King's Arms Tavern Creamed Onions with Peanuts**
	*King's Arms Tavern Sweet Potatoes**
Salad	*Fresh Garden Stuff*
Bread	*Sally Lunn**
	*Indian Corn Sticks**

SECOND COURSE
*Pecan Pie**

A New Year's Eve Cocktail Party

*Chilled Backfin Crabmeat with Mayonnaise**
*Cheddar Cheese and Olive Balls**
*Barbecued Baby Spareribs**
*Marinated Shrimp in Fresh Dill**
*Skewered Pineapple and Strawberries in Kirsch**
*Biscuits Spread with Virginia Ham Pâté**

16

* *Recipe is in this cookbook; see index for page number.*

Tavern Fare

Christiana Campbell's Tavern

Mrs. Christiana Campbell kept the tavern that bears her name from 1771 to 1776. From a contemporary description it seems that Mrs. Campbell was certainly no beauty, but she was an excellent manager and had a way of knowing and remembering just what each patron especially liked. George Washington, then a burgess, recorded that he had dined at Mrs. Campbell's twenty-seven times during one session of the General Assembly, and supped and spent many an evening besides under her roof. Among Colonial Williamsburg's prized possessions is a receipt for payment for food and drink given by George Washington to Christiana Campbell on April 8, 1772.

Situated behind the Capitol, Christiana Campbell's Tavern today features seafood from the Chesapeake Bay.

Bill of Fare at Christiana Campbell's Tavern

Bill of FARE

Fresh Melon with Surry County Ham

| Clams from the Eastern Shore | Captain Rasmussen's Clam Chowder |
| Chesapeake Bay Oysters (in season) | French Onion Soup with Croutons |

Chilled Crabmeat Cocktail with Fresh Horseradish

* * * * * * *

Platter of Assorted Seafoods,
Fried Chesapeake Bay Oysters, Carolina Shrimp, and Scallops combined with Virginia Fish and Crab Imperial. Broiled Tomato.

A Made Dish of Shrimp and Lobster,
A Casserole of Shrimp and Lobster combined with Fresh Mushrooms, Tomatoes, Green Pepper, Onion, and Sherry. Served on Wild Rice.

Hampton Crab Imperial,
Freshly Picked Lump Crabmeat seasoned and baked in the Natural Shell. Fried Potatoes.

Fresh Fish from Virginia Waters,
Broiled to Your Liking. Fried Potatoes.

Roast Young Urbanna Duckling,
Seasoned with Apples and Onions and served with Wild Rice.

Twenty Ounce T-Bone,
Garnished with Braised Sliced Mushrooms and Fried Potatoes.

Colonial Game Pie,
Braised Venison, Duck, and Rabbit with Fresh Mushrooms, Bacon Lardoons, and Currant Jelly. Served with Wild Rice.

Tenderloin of Beef Bound with Bacon,
Garnished with Braised Sliced Mushrooms and Fried Potatoes.

(Cole Slaw or Watercress Salad served with Entree)

* * * * * * *

| Corn Sticks | Biscuits | Spoon Bread |

* * * * * * *

Campbell's Fig Ice Cream

Vanilla or Chocolate Ice Cream	Rum Cream Pie—Chocolate Curls
Warm Apple Turnover with Nutmeg Sauce	Tipsy Squire with Whipped Cream and Almonds
Raspberry Sherbet	Pears and Port Wine

* * * * * * *

| Tea | Coffee | Milk |

King's Arms Tavern

Mrs. Jane Vobe kept tavern at various locations in Williamsburg for thirty-three years, longer, so far as is known, than anyone else. First recorded as keeping tavern in 1752, she opened a new tavern "at the sign of the King's Arms" on Duke of Gloucester Street in 1772, and presumably retired in 1785, when she advertised the King's Arms for rent. She sold tickets for theater performances, invited artists to display their pictures in the tavern, posted rewards for the return of articles lost by guests, and prided herself on attracting a clientele as select as any in town.

The present-day King's Arms continues to serve the best. Here Colonial Williamsburg has entertained among others the king and queen of Thailand, the lord mayor of London and his lady, the president of the Argentine Republic, England's Queen Mother Elizabeth, and King Baudouin of the Belgians.

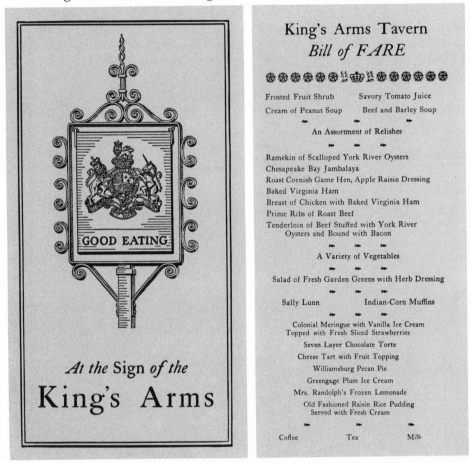

At the Sign *of the*

King's Arms

King's Arms Tavern
Bill of FARE

Frosted Fruit Shrub   Savory Tomato Juice
Cream of Peanut Soup   Beef and Barley Soup

An Assortment of Relishes

Ramekin of Scalloped York River Oysters
Chesapeake Bay Jambalaya
Roast Cornish Game Hen, Apple Raisin Dressing
Baked Virginia Ham
Breast of Chicken with Baked Virginia Ham
Prime Ribs of Roast Beef
Tenderloin of Beef Stuffed with York River
    Oysters and Bound with Bacon

A Variety of Vegetables

Salad of Fresh Garden Greens with Herb Dressing

Sally Lunn   Indian-Corn Muffins

Colonial Meringue with Vanilla Ice Cream
Topped with Fresh Sliced Strawberries
Seven Layer Chocolate Torte
Cheese Tart with Fruit Topping
Williamsburg Pecan Pie
Greengage Plum Ice Cream
Mrs. Randolph's Frozen Lemonade
Old Fashioned Raisin Rice Pudding
Served with Fresh Cream

Coffee   Tea   Milk

Chowning's Tavern

Josiah Chowning opened his tavern in 1766 for humbler folk or ordinary people, as he put it, assuring them they could "depend upon the best of Entertainment for Themselves, Servants and Horses, and good pasturage." He prided himself on his good bread. On Chowning's bill of fare the word "sippets" describes strips of dry toast. The sandwiches are made from hand-sliced bread, which is why a neighbor's sandwich may be slightly thicker or thinner than your own.

Chowning's Tavern retains much of its original character, that of an alehouse of old. Of the three taverns, its atmosphere is nearest to that of an English village pub. Draft ale, beer, and other spiritous beverages are served. Students from the College of William and Mary like to go there for "Chowning's good Bread"(a loaf-sized round)with butter and a glass of cider—served ice cold in summer under the grapevine-covered arbor, or mulled and spiced in winter before the fireplace.

Chowning's Tavern Evening Fare

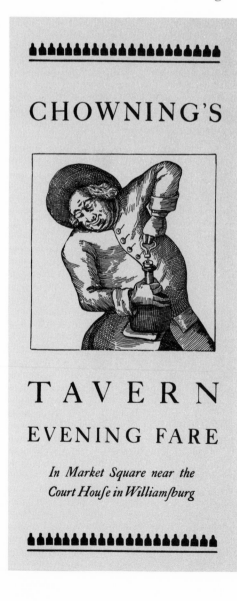

CHOWNING'S

TAVERN

EVENING FARE

In Market Square near the Court House in Williamsburg

EVENING FARE

Tomato Juice Cocktail

Leek and Potato Soup

Clams on the Shell from the Eastern Shore

Oysters on the Shell (in the Proper Seasons) from the Chesapeake Bay

Brunswick Stew

Made from Young Fowl and Fresh Garden Stuff, seasoned to Taste, and served Hot with Chowning's Good Bread and Butter and Garden Salad

Welsh Rabbit with Surry County Ham

Melted Snappy Cheese blended with Beer and Seasoning on Toasted Bread, served Hot with a Garden Salad

Chowning's Barbecued Backribs

Broiled Backribs braised in a Barbecue Sauce, Chowning's Bread and Butter, Baked Potato and a Garden Salad

Backfin Chesapeake Bay Crabmeat, Saute

Local Backfin Crabmeat sauted in Shallot Butter, served with Chowning's Bread and Butter, Baked Potato and a Garden Salad

Majestic Roast Prime Ribs of Beef

Cut to your liking — Rare — Medium — Well Done

Served up with a Baked Potato, Chowning's Good Bread and Butter and a Garden Salad

Desserts

Buttered Apple Pie, made with Apples from the Shenandoah Valley of Virginia

Served with a Wedge of Old Cheddar Cheese or Vanilla Ice Cream

Chowning's Black Walnut Ice Cream

Orange Nut Pound Cake

Served with Vanilla Ice Cream

Vanilla Ice Cream

Pecan Tart

Beverages

Coffee or Tea, Hot or Iced

Milk

Part II

Recipes

Appetizers

The appetizer, which came in with Prohibition to accompany what was often an unpalatable drink and stayed on in favor as companion to the cocktail, nowadays takes first place on the menu, and is a new course.

BARBECUED BABY SPARERIBS

(4–6 servings)

5 pounds baby spareribs
salt and pepper to taste

curry powder
BARBECUE SAUCE *(page 91)*

Preheat oven to 400° F.

Prepare spareribs by removing excess fat and cutting into as many pieces as desired.

Place flesh side up on a rack in a shallow roasting pan.

Sprinkle with salt and pepper and very lightly with curry powder.

Cook spareribs at 400° F. for 1 hour, brushing with warm Barbecue Sauce every 10 minutes.

When spareribs are cooked, baste with remaining Barbecue Sauce and serve.

CHEDDAR CHEESE AND OLIVE BALLS

(36–40 balls)

¼ pound Cheddar cheese
¼ cup butter, softened
¼ teaspoon paprika

¾ cup all-purpose flour
36 to 40 tiny stuffed Spanish
olives, drained

Preheat oven to 375° F.

Grate cheese and allow to soften to room temperature.

Combine cheese, butter, and paprika.

Mix well into flour, by hand, until pieces of cheese disappear and mixture is smooth and deep yellow in color.

Cover and allow to stand at room temperature 15 minutes.

Pinch off small pieces of dough (about 1 teaspoon) and flatten in palm of hand to a circle about 1½ inches in diameter.

Place well-drained olive in center of dough, bringing edges together to cover olive completely. Roll gently between palms of hands.

Place on ungreased cookie sheet; chill 10 minutes in refrigerator.

Bake at 375° F. for 20 to 25 minutes, or until lightly browned. Serve hot.

Note: May be made in advance and frozen before baking. Bake frozen, about 30 minutes. Do not thaw.

CHEESE WAFERS

(3 dozen)

1 cup all-purpose flour
1 teaspoon salt
½ teaspoon ginger
⅓ cup shortening
1 cup grated sharp cheese, packed

¼ cup toasted sesame seeds
½ teaspoon Worcestershire sauce
2 to 3 tablespoons ice water

Preheat oven to 400° F. 10 minutes before wafers are to go in. Grease cookie sheets.

Combine all ingredients and work into smooth dough.

Divide the dough in half, making 2 rolls about 8 inches long and 1¼ inches in diameter, and put them in the refrigerator to chill.

When firm slice into wafers ⅛ inch thick.

Place on prepared cookie sheets and prick with a fork.

Bake at 400° F. for 10 to 12 minutes.

CHICKEN TURNOVERS

(6 large or 12 cocktail)

1 egg, beaten, divided
2 tablespoons milk
1 cup cooked chicken, ground
¼ teaspoon salt
white pepper to taste
⅛ teaspoon leaf thyme or poultry seasoning

½ cup chicken gravy or condensed cream of chicken soup
1 tablespoon pimiento, chopped
PASTRY CRUST MIX *(page 131)* as needed

Preheat oven to 350° F.

Grease a cookie sheet.

Beat egg and remove 1 tablespoon to mix with milk for egg wash.

Make filling by combining chicken, remaining egg, salt, pepper, thyme or poultry seasoning, gravy or condensed cream of chicken soup, and pimiento.

Roll out pastry on lightly floured board and cut into rounds 3 inches in diameter for cocktail size and 6 inches in diameter for large size.

Spoon 1 slightly rounded tablespoon of filling onto ½ of each small round, 2 tablespoons on the large rounds, and fold over other half of the round. Press edges together with a fork dipped in milk.

Brush with egg wash and place on prepared cookie sheet.

Bake at 350° F. for 20 to 25 minutes.

SHRIMP TURNOVERS

(6 large or 12 cocktail)

1 egg, beaten, divided
2 tablespoons milk
10 ounces cooked shrimp, ground
salt and pepper to taste

⅛ teaspoon dill seed or seafood seasoning
2 tablespoons mayonnaise
2 tablespoons lemon juice
PASTRY CRUST MIX *(page 131)*, as needed

Follow instructions for Chicken Turnovers (page 24).

Note: The large turnovers can be served as a main course with hot Cheese Sauce (page 93).

CHILLED BACKFIN CRABMEAT WITH MAYONNAISE

(4–6 servings)

1 pound backfin crabmeat
2 tablespoons lemon juice
salt and pepper to taste

½ cup mayonnaise
1 head lettuce (Boston or Bibb)

Pick over chilled crabmeat and discard any bits of shell or cartilage.

Season with lemon juice, salt and pepper.

Gently fold in mayonnaise.

Serve on lettuce cups.

MARINATED SHRIMP IN FRESH DILL

(8–10 servings)

1 teaspoon dill seed	2½ pounds shrimp in shell
1 lemon, sliced	MARINADE OF FRESH DILL
	(below)

Bring salted water, dill seed, and sliced lemon to boil.

Add shrimp and simmer until the shrimp are pink, about 3 to 4 minutes.

Immediately drain and chill the shrimp.

Peel and devein shrimp and place them in a crock or bowl.

Pour Marinade of Fresh Dill over shrimp; cover and store in refrigerator for 24 hours.

MARINADE OF FRESH DILL

½ cup olive oil	dash of garlic powder
½ cup dry white wine	2 drops Tabasco sauce
4 teaspoons fresh dill, chopped	½ cup lemon juice
1 teaspoon fresh cracked	salt to taste
pepper	1 tablespoon chives

Mix all ingredients well.

Appetizers

MELON BALLS WITH VIRGINIA HAM
(24–36 balls)

6 to 8 ounces VIRGINIA HAM
(page 45), very thinly sliced

*1 medium honeydew, large
cantaloupe or Spanish melon*

Slice ham into thin strips about 1 inch wide by 4 inches long.

Cut melon into balls using No. 25 melon-ball cutter (approximately 1 inch in diameter).

Place melon balls on cheesecloth or paper toweling to absorb moisture.

Wrap each melon ball with a strip of ham secured with a toothpick.

Chill and serve.

OYSTERS WITH BACON
(1 dozen)

6 slices bacon
12 fresh oysters
*1 teaspoon Worcestershire
sauce*

salt and pepper to taste
1 tablespoon lemon juice

Preheat oven to 400° F.

Cut bacon strips in half and cook until partially done; drain.

Season oysters and wrap each oyster in half a slice of bacon; secure with a toothpick.

Bake at 400° F. on a rack over a shallow pan for 5 to 7 minutes, or until bacon is done. Serve hot.

SKEWERED PINEAPPLE
AND STRAWBERRIES IN KIRSCH
(8–10 servings)

1 fresh pineapple, well ripened
*1 quart (40 to 50) fresh
strawberries*

½ cup kirsch
bamboo skewers as needed
crushed ice

Peel and cube fresh pineapple.

Pick over strawberries, wash, and hull.

Place pineapple cubes and strawberries in bowl; sprinkle with kirsch.

Chill at least 30 minutes, turning several times.

To serve, place pineapple and strawberries alternately on skewers.

Place skewers over crushed ice in glass bowl to keep chilled for serving.

VIRGINIA HAM BISCUITS

(40 regular or 70 cocktail)

milk
1 recipe Mrs. Booth's Biscuit Mix *(page 111)*

melted butter
1¼ to 1½ pounds Virginia Ham *(page 45), very thinly sliced*

Preheat oven to 425° F.

Grease cookie sheets.

Using a fork, stir enough milk into biscuit mix to make a soft but not sticky dough.

Knead on lightly floured board until dough is smooth and elastic.

Roll out ¼ inch thick, then fold dough over so that biscuits will open easily when baked.

Cut with 1½- or 2-inch biscuit cutter, place on prepared cookie sheets, and brush tops with melted butter or milk.

Bake at 425° F. for 8 to 10 minutes or until golden brown.

Place pieces of ham in biscuits and serve warm.

Note: Biscuits and ham can be put together ahead of time, wrapped in aluminum foil, and reheated for serving.

BISCUITS SPREAD
WITH VIRGINIA HAM PATE

(40 regular or 70 cocktail)

milk
1 recipe MRS. BOOTH'S BISCUIT
  MIX *(page 111)*
melted butter
¼ cup French-style prepared
  mustard

½ cup mayonnaise
1 pound VIRGINIA HAM *(page*
  45), finely ground

Follow instructions under Virginia Ham Biscuits (page 28) to make the biscuits.

Add mustard and mayonnaise to very finely ground ham; mix thoroughly.

Spread on hot biscuits; serve warm.

Note: As an alternative serving suggestion, the ham mixture may be rolled into small balls (about 1 teaspoon) with a peanut in the center, rolled in fine bread crumbs, and fried quickly in deep hot fat until golden brown. Drain well and serve warm.

Soups and Stews

An "excellent Soupe" made of venison and turkey moved William Byrd II to an unusual metaphor: "It never cloy'd, no more than an Engaging Wife wou'd do, by being a Constant Dish."

Eighteenth-century men were not the only admirers of good soup. President Harry S. Truman, who visited Williamsburg during his years in the White House, liked the soup served him at the Inn so well that he sent a message of congratulations to the chef. "One day I'll slip back for more—only nobody will know I'm here."

Soups are, broadly speaking, either thick or clear. In colonial days thick soups were favored. Modern gastronomes would call for a consommé or clear soup for a festive dinner.

A Williamsburg guest in 1946, Sir Winston Churchill so liked the Clear Green Turtle Soup Amontillado served him at the dinner in his honor at the Inn that he asked for more. Resting afterward in his room before boarding an after-midnight special train to take him back to Washington, he asked if a tureen of the same turtle consommé could be sent up to his room. The kitchen was closed, but the chef was still around, and soon a full tureen was sent to the statesman's room.

A decade later, the same Clear Green Turtle Soup Amontillado Sir Winston Churchill so relished was served at the Inn to Queen Elizabeth and Prince Philip.

When asked for the secret of his good soups, Fred Crawford, chef at the Inn for many years, replied instantly, "It's the way the ingredients are put together and the seasonings." This was, perhaps, an oversimplified way of saying that nothing can be taken out of a pot which does not first go in. If the base of a soup is not just right, no amount of boiling and simmering can put it right. The art of cookery lies in the blending and proportions of the seasonings.

CLEAR GREEN TURTLE SOUP AMONTILLADO

(12–15 servings)

Bouquet garni:
   ½ teaspoon sweet basil
   ½ teaspoon marjoram
   ½ teaspoon rosemary
   ½ teaspoon thyme
   ½ teaspoon fennel seeds
   ½ teaspoon mint
   ½ teaspoon sage
   ½ teaspoon allspice

1 jar (2¼ ounces) beef-flavored instant bouillon beads
1 can (28 ounces) green turtle meat
salt and pepper to taste
1 cup amontillado sherry

Prepare bouquet garni by tying herbs in a cheesecloth bag.

Dissolve the bouillon beads in 1 gallon water, bring to a boil, and turn heat to simmer.

Add the bouquet garni and simmer 15 minutes.

Drain the juice from the turtle meat and reserve; add juices to stock.

Simmer at least 30 minutes, skimming froth from stock occasionally.

Cut cold turtle meat into small cubes.

Remove stock from heat and strain through a double thickness of cheesecloth. Return to heat, add turtle meat and salt and pepper to taste.

Add the sherry to taste, about 1 tablespoon, to each individual portion before serving.

ESSENCE OF TOMATO

(6–8 servings)

1 pound ground beef
1 soup bone
2 cups (1 pound) canned tomatoes
3 ribs of celery, chopped, divided
1 large onion, sliced

2 cups tomato juice
½ teaspoon pickling spice
1 large bay leaf
½ cup carrots, finely chopped
½ cup green beans, finely chopped
salt to taste

Put meat, bone, and tomatoes in a kettle with 4 quarts water.
Chop celery, reserving ½ cup.

Add remaining celery, onion, tomato juice, and spices to mixture in kettle.

Bring to boil, then simmer, uncovered, for 3 hours, reducing liquid to about 2 quarts.

In a separate saucepan, cook carrots, green beans and reserved celery in 2 cups of the soup broth.

When vegetables are cooked, strain and return the broth to the soup kettle.

Strain soup through a double thickness of cheesecloth.

Salt to taste and garnish with cooked vegetables.

Serve hot or cold.

BEEF BROTH
WITH TOMATOES AND OKRA

(6 servings)

1 soup bone	*pinch of leaf oregano*
1 pound ground beef	*3 cups canned tomatoes*
1 pound stewing beef	*1 cup okra, cut*
3 ribs of celery with leaves,	*2 tablespoons cornstarch*
* chopped*	*salt and pepper to taste*
2 medium onions, sliced	*dash of Worcestershire sauce*
1 large bay leaf	

Put soup bone, ground beef, stewing meat, celery, onions, bay leaf, and oregano in a kettle with 2 quarts water and simmer for 1½ hours uncovered.

Remove and dice stewing beef.

Strain the stock. Skim off fat.

Add the diced stewing beef, tomatoes, and okra to the strained stock and return to heat.

Mix cornstarch with a little cold water and stir into stock until evenly blended.

Add seasonings and cook uncovered for 20 minutes.

Serve very hot.

KING'S ARMS TAVERN
CREAM OF PEANUT SOUP

(10–12 servings)

Brazil is the native home of the peanut, the "ground nut" that sailed with Portuguese explorers to Africa and back to the Americas with the Negro. In 1794, Thomas Jefferson recorded the yield of sixty-five peanut hills at Monticello. The cultivation of peanuts increased in the South in the nineteenth century, but it was not until after the Civil War that they gained national acceptance.

Peanut soup is comparatively new, but it is much in demand in King's Arms Tavern.

1 medium onion, chopped
2 ribs of celery, chopped
¼ cup butter
3 tablespoons all-purpose flour
2 quarts CHICKEN STOCK *(page 43) or canned chicken broth*

2 cups smooth peanut butter
1¾ cups light cream
peanuts, chopped

Sauté onion and celery in butter until soft, but not brown.
Stir in flour until well blended.
Add Chicken Stock, stirring constantly, and bring to a boil.
Remove from heat and rub through a sieve.
Add peanut butter and cream, stirring to blend thoroughly.
Return to low heat, but do not boil, and serve, garnished with peanuts.
Note: This soup is also good served ice cold.

BISQUE OF HAMPTON CRAB

(6 servings)

Hampton Roads, at the mouth of the James River, is the chief anchorage for the ports of Norfolk, Portsmouth, and Newport News, which surround it. At times, it is said, the Roads have been so crowded with cargo vessels that one could cross the waterway by walking from deck to deck, though there is no record of anyone trying it. Shellfish, among them crabs, flourished in abundance in earlier years along the bottom of Hampton Roads, unheeding of the bustle overhead.

1 cup crabmeat
1 can condensed cream of mushroom soup
1 can condensed cream of asparagus soup
1 cup light cream

1¼ cup milk
½ teaspoon Worcestershire sauce
⅛ teaspoon Tabasco sauce
⅓ cup dry sherry

Pick over crabmeat and remove any bits of shell or cartilage.
Place the crabmeat and soups into a blender container or mixer bowl; mix well.
Pour into a saucepan, add remaining ingredients, and heat just until hot, not boiling.

BISQUE OF CLAM AND CHICKEN

(4–6 servings)

1½ cups clam juice
2 tablespoons onion, finely chopped
¼ cup celery, diced
1 small bay leaf
2 cups CHICKEN STOCK (page 43), or canned chicken broth
2 tablespoons butter
3 tablespoons all-purpose flour

1 cup cooked chicken, finely chopped
½ cup clams, finely chopped
1 cup light cream
salt and white pepper to taste
¼ cup whipping cream
1 tablespoon pimiento, drained and finely chopped

Simmer clam juice with onion, celery, and bay leaf for 30 minutes.
Add Chicken Stock and bring to a boil.
Strain and discard vegetables and bay leaf.
Melt butter in medium-sized saucepan and blend in flour.
Add hot stock all at once, stirring vigorously until evenly blended.

34

Add chicken, clams, and light cream.

Salt and pepper to taste.

Simmer 20 minutes over low heat, but do not boil, stirring occasionally.

Whip cream until soft peaks form.

Fold in well-drained pimiento.

Serve bisque in warm bowls with 1 tablespoon of whipped cream-pimiento mixture on each serving.

Note: This bisque is very rich—servings will be small.

WILLIAMSBURG INN CHILLED CRAB GUMBO

(12 servings)

Bouquet garni:
  6 parsley stems, chopped
  1 clove garlic, minced
  ½ teaspoon leaf thyme
  ½ teaspoon leaf marjoram
  2 bay leaves
½ cup celery, finely chopped
½ cup onions, finely chopped
½ cup green pepper, finely chopped
½ cup leeks, finely chopped
1 pound crabmeat, cooked

pinch of saffron
1 cup okra, chopped (see note below)
1 cup tomatoes, chopped
1 teaspoon salt or to taste
½ teaspoon white pepper
½ teaspoon gumbo filé powder (see note below)
1 envelope unflavored gelatin softened in ½ cup warm water
1 cup rice, cooked

Prepare bouquet garni by tying herbs in a cheesecloth bag.

Heat 2 quarts water (or fish stock) to boiling, add bouquet garni, celery, onions, green pepper, and leeks.

Cover and simmer 20 minutes.

Pick over crabmeat and remove any bits of shell or cartilage.

Add crabmeat and saffron to simmering vegetables and continue to simmer slowly for 15 minutes.

Add okra, tomatoes, salt, and pepper.

Remove ½ cup liquid from pot, sprinkle in filé powder, and beat thoroughly.

Stir into pot. *Be careful not to let the soup boil after the filé powder has been added or it will become stringy and unfit to serve.*

Remove from heat and stir in softened gelatin.

Add cooked rice and adjust seasoning.

Refrigerate overnight if possible to bring out flavor.

Serve in cold cups.

Note: If canned okra is used the liquid may be added to the gumbo after the cooking process as it will enhance the flavor of the soup. If raw okra is used, blanch it in 2 cups of the stock before adding with the tomatoes.

Also note: Okra will take the place of filé powder if the latter is not available; however, gumbo tastes best when both okra and filé powder are used.

CHOWNING'S TAVERN BRUNSWICK STEW

(8–10 servings)

By all accounts, every place named Brunswick from Canada to the Carolinas has tried to claim this stew as its own. There have also been as many arguments about what precisely went into the original pot, and what should go in now.

All in all, Brunswick County, Virginia, has the best claim to being the birthplace of this popular dish that in its heyday was served at all of Virginia's tobacco-curings and public gatherings. The story goes that a hunting party in Brunswick County, well provisioned with tomatoes, onions, cabbage, butter beans, red pepper, bacon, salt, and corn, left one man behind to mind the commissary and to have dinner ready at day's end. Disgruntled, he shot a squirrel, the only thing he could find within range of the camp, and threw it into the pot along with the vegetables. When it was served, everybody agreed that squirrel, one of the finest and tenderest of all wild meats, was what made the new stew just right. Chicken is now substituted.

1 *stewing hen (6 pounds), or*
  2 broiler-fryers (3 pounds
  each)
2 *large onions, sliced*
2 *cups okra, cut (optional)*
4 *cups fresh or 2 cans (1 pound*
  each) tomatoes
2 *cups lima beans*
3 *medium potatoes, diced*
4 *cups corn cut from cob* or
  2 cans (1 pound each) corn
3 *teaspoons salt*
1 *teaspoon pepper*
1 *tablespoon sugar*

Cut chicken in pieces and simmer in 3 quarts water for a thin stew, or 2 quarts for a thick stew, until meat can easily be removed from bones, about 2¼ hours.

Add raw vegetables to broth and simmer, uncovered, until beans and potatoes are tender.

Stir occasionally to prevent scorching.

Add chicken, boned and diced if desired, and the seasonings.

Note: If canned vegetables are used, include juices and reduce water to 2 quarts for a thin stew, 1 quart for a thick stew.

Also note: Brunswick Stew is one of those delectable things that benefit from long, slow cooking. It is a rule in some tidewater homes never to eat Brunswick Stew the same day it is made as its flavor improves if it is left to stand overnight and reheated.

OUTER BANKS CLAM CHOWDER

(6 servings)

Originally chowder was a fisherman's stew of French origin, with salt pork or bacon being as essential an ingredient as the fish. New Englanders probably got their early recipe for chowder from French settlers in Canada; Virginians got it more likely from the English, whose cookbooks contained recipes for "chouder, a sea dish." For some time now, corn and other ingredients have supplemented the fish, and chowderlike thick soups of meat and vegetables have also developed.

12 *large clams*
¼ pound fat bacon or *salt pork*
2 *medium onions, sliced fine*
3 *medium potatoes, cubed*

salt and white pepper to taste
2 *tablespoons corn meal* or
   all-purpose flour
1 *cup light cream*

Scrub clams and boil in enough water to cover.

Remove clams from shells, chop fine, reserve.

Strain liquid and add enough water to make 6 cups, reserve.

Cut bacon in very small pieces or, if using pork, into ½-inch cubes.

Fry until crisp and brown.

Add onions, potatoes, clams, and reserved liquid; simmer until potatoes are done.

Season with salt and pepper.

Mix corn meal or flour in a little cold water and stir into chowder.

Add cream.

Serve at once in warm bowls.

Note: When fresh clams are not available, 2 bottles (8 ounces each) clam juice and 2 cans (7½ to 8 ounces each) minced clams and their liquid can be substituted.

CHESAPEAKE OYSTER BISQUE

(*8–10 servings*)

1 *quart oysters*
1 *bay leaf*
2 *medium onions, chopped*
   and divided
2 *ribs of celery, chopped and*
   divided
½ *cup butter*

¼ cup all-purpose flour
½ *teaspoon salt*
¼ teaspoon white pepper
1 *pint light cream*
¼ cup dry sherry (*optional*)
paprika or *parsley*

Drain and chop oysters; reserve.

Add enough water to drained oyster liquor to make 2 quarts.

Add bay leaf, 1 onion, and 1 rib of celery and simmer uncovered for 30 minutes.

Remove from heat and allow to "ripen" at least an hour, then strain.

38

Melt butter in saucepan and add remaining onion and celery. Sauté 5 minutes.

Stir in flour but do not brown; remove from heat and add part of the oyster stock, stirring constantly.

Return to heat and add remaining stock, stirring until smooth.

Add salt and pepper and cook over low heat 10 minutes.

Add oysters and cream; simmer gently 2 or 3 minutes.

If sherry is to be added, do so just before serving in warm bowls.

Garnish with paprika or chopped parsley.

CREAM OF OYSTER AND SPINACH SOUP

(12–16 servings)

1½ quarts oysters
2 pounds frozen chopped
   spinach
6 tablespoons butter
⅔ cup onion, coarsely chopped
2 ribs of celery, very finely
   chopped
6 tablespoons all-purpose flour

½ teaspoon garlic salt
pinch nutmeg
2 tablespoons steak sauce
salt and pepper to taste
1 quart milk
1 quart light cream
whipped cream

Cook oysters in 3 cups of water until well done or firm; drain liquid, keep hot.

Purée oysters in blender or pass through sieve.

Cook spinach until well done; drain well. Purée in blender or pass through sieve.

Melt butter over medium heat; cook onions and celery, stirring constantly.

Push onions and celery to one side of pan; sprinkle flour over butter and stir to make a paste.

Pour in hot oyster liquid, whipping to make smooth. Cook, uncovered, for 30 minutes. Strain.

Return to heat and simmer.

Add puréed oysters and spinach to simmering liquid.

Add garlic salt, nutmeg, steak sauce, and salt and pepper to taste.

Add milk and cream and continue to cook over low heat for 5 to 10 minutes, but do not boil.

Serve hot topped with whipped cream.

OYSTER STEW

(4 servings)

1 pint oysters	*dash Tabasco sauce*
4 tablespoons butter, divided	*1 pint milk*
¾ teaspoon salt	*1 pint light cream*
pepper to taste	*paprika*

Drain oysters and reserve liquor.

Melt all but 2 teaspoons of butter over medium heat and add salt, pepper, and Tabasco sauce.

Add oyster liquor to butter and seasonings; stir to blend.

Add oysters and cook only until edges begin to curl.

Stir in milk and cream and bring almost to the boiling point.

Serve in hot bowls, top with remaining butter, and sprinkle with paprika.

CASCADES TURTLE GUMBO

(12–15 servings)

¼ cup vegetable oil	*1 tablespoon Worcestershire sauce*
2 cups onion, coarsely chopped	*pinch cayenne pepper*
4 ribs of celery, cut in 1-inch pieces	*2 pounds turtle meat, coarsely chopped*
2 green peppers, coarsely chopped	*1½ cups okra, cooked (see note below)*
1 clove garlic, minced	*1 cup long-grain rice, cooked*
1 gallon TURTLE STOCK *(page 41)*	*salt and pepper to taste*
1 bottle (8 ounces) clam juice	*1 teaspoon gumbo filé powder (see note below)*
1 cup tomato purée	
2 cups whole plum tomatoes, diced	

Heat the oil in a large pot.

Sauté the onion, celery, and green peppers until almost tender.

Add the garlic and cook 1 more minute, stirring constantly.

Add Turtle Stock, clam juice, and tomato purée; bring to a boil then reduce heat immediately.

Simmer 15 minutes and add the tomatoes, Worcestershire sauce, cayenne pepper, and the turtle meat.

Cook, uncovered, 15 minutes.

Add okra, rice, and salt and pepper to taste.

Remove ½ cup stock, sprinkle with filé powder, and beat until smooth.

Return to the pot and stir well, *but be careful not to let the stock boil after the filé powder has been added or it will become stringy and unfit to serve.*

Note: If canned okra is used the liquid can be added to the gumbo after the cooking process to enhance the flavor of the soup.

Also note: Okra will take the place of filé powder if the latter is not available; however, gumbo tastes better when both okra and filé powder are used.

TURTLE STOCK

(*1¼ gallons*)

2½ to 3 pounds turtle meat, tied in cheesecloth	*1 bay leaf*
2 cups onion, chopped	*6 peppercorns*
3 ribs of celery, cut in 1-inch pieces	*6 cloves*
2 carrots, sliced	*2½ cups whole plum tomatoes with liquid*
pinch of leaf thyme	*1 cup tomato purée*

Combine all of the above ingredients with 1½ gallons of water in a large pot, and allow to come to a boil.

Reduce heat and simmer, partially covered, approximately 1½ hours.

Check turtle meat to see if it comes easily from the bones. If it does, remove it from the stock and reserve. If not, allow stock to simmer a few more minutes.

Continue cooking the stock, uncovered, for 30 minutes.
Pick turtle meat from the bones for use in gumbo.
Strain stock through cheesecloth.

WILLIAMSBURG LODGE
CORN CHOWDER

(6 servings)

3 ounces salt pork, cubed
1 large onion, chopped
1 rib of celery, chopped
1½ cups potatoes, diced
2 cups CHICKEN STOCK *(page 43), or canned chicken broth*

2 cups cream-style corn
2 cups milk
¼ cup butter
salt and white pepper to taste

Fry pork until brown.

Add onion and cook over medium heat 5 minutes, stirring often.

Add celery, potatoes, Chicken Stock, and 1 cup water and cook until potatoes are done.

Add corn and heat 5 minutes, stirring occasionally.

Heat milk and butter and add to the soup.

Salt and pepper to taste and serve hot.

BEEF STOCK

(2–3 quarts)

10 pounds beef bones (shanks or whatever is available)
¼ cup vegetable oil
3 medium onions, chopped
2 ribs of celery, chopped
2 carrots, chopped
2 cloves garlic

1½ cups whole canned tomatoes
½ cup tomato purée
½ teaspoon leaf thyme
½ teaspoon black pepper
1 bay leaf

Preheat oven to 400° F.

42

Saw beef bones in half or ask the butcher to do it. Place them in a roasting pan and brown well in the oven at 400° F., approximately 45 minutes.

Remove from oven, drain fat, and place bones in a large soup pot.

Heat oil in a black iron skillet. Add onion, celery, carrots, and garlic.

Allow vegetables to brown thoroughly, but do not burn.

Remove the oil, and add the browned vegetables, tomatoes, tomato purée, and seasonings to the pot of bones.

Cover with cold water and bring to a boil. Reduce heat and simmer uncovered for 6 to 8 hours.

Strain stock through a double thickness of cheesecloth.

Note: Stock can be frozen in cubes for future use.

CHICKEN STOCK

(4 quarts)

Bouquet garni:
  ½ teaspoon leaf thyme
  1 small bay leaf
  ½ teaspoon leaf marjoram
  3 sprigs parsley
  6 peppercorns
2 medium onions
3 to 4 ribs of celery, including
  leaves

3 to 4 carrots, washed but
  not scraped
2 to 3 leeks or *spring onions,*
  including green tops
4 to 5 pounds chicken necks,
  backs, and wings
1 tablespoon salt
1 cup dry white wine
  (optional)

Prepare bouquet garni by tying herbs in a cheesecloth bag. Cut vegetables into 1-inch pieces.

Place all ingredients into a large soup pot with enough water to cover them by at least 2 inches.

Bring to a boil over medium heat. Partially cover and simmer for 2 to 3 hours, or until chicken comes easily from bones; remove.

Remove cover and continue to simmer stock over low heat until it is reduced to about 4 quarts.

Strain stock, refrigerate, and when cold, remove all fat.

Note: Stock can be frozen in cubes for future use.

Meats

Since beef cattle roamed until they were lean and tough, veal and pork were the most popular domestic meats in eighteenth-century Virginia. Not until about the 1890s did grain-fed beef find wide acceptance in the diet of Virginians. Pork, and above all ham, held its favored place on the bills of fare over the centuries. Epicurean Virginians rarely mentioned ham in diaries because there was no Virginian of consequence who did not have ham on his table at all times, with other meats of course.

Beef is beef and pork is pork wherever they come from, but Virginia ham is about as different from most other hams as chalk is from cheese. Unlike the pinkish, soft meat of ordinary hams, the truly aged Virginia ham is of a rich mahogany color, firm, and highly flavored. To be served properly, it should be cut paper thin.

The pig of the early Tidewater, left to forage in the forests for its food, grew into a smaller and leaner hog than his pen-fed descendents. The half-wild porkers multiplied so rapidly that as early as 1639 ham and bacon were being shipped to England. Because of climate and the long voyage by sailing ship, proper curing was of prime importance. The slow smoking over smoldering hickory wood and the months of undisturbed aging gave the hams a distinctive flavor that rivaled Europe's best. Hugh Jones wrote in 1724, "The hams being scarce to be distinguished from those of Westphalia."

The curing and shipping of Virginia hams gradually became concentrated in the counties of Suffolk and Surry, south of the James River. Smithfield, which became the Virginia ham capital, was named not for London's famous meat market but for Arthur Smith, on whose land the town was founded in 1752. Luckily the soil, which was too poor for tobacco growing, proved ideal for growing peanuts, and peanuts are a crop that hogs relish.

44

Nowadays, instead of running wild in the forests, the hogs are turned loose to glean the vast peanut-growing acreages below the James River where ripe, unroasted peanuts remain after harvesting. The distinctive flavor that is produced by the combination of diet and cure has remained a favorite for generations. Britain's Queen Victoria had a regular order for the hams of the peanut-fed hogs. During her visit in 1957, Queen Elizabeth liked Virginia ham so well that her host, Winthrop Rockefeller, ordered a ham sent to her in London.

VIRGINIA HAM AND BRANDIED PEACHES

Williamsburg visitors who plan to carry home a Virginia ham as a souvenir are advised to heed these preliminary directions or they may be sadly disappointed:

Scrub the ham to remove the coating of seasonings; cover it with water and soak for 24 hours.

Place the ham, skin side down, in a pan with enough fresh water to cover; bring to a boil, then reduce heat and simmer, covered, for 20 to 25 minutes per pound.

When done, skin the ham and trim off excess fat.

Note: These directions apply to a Virginia ham that has been cured for at least 12 months. If the ham has been cured less than 12 months, follow instructions on the wrapper or hang the ham and allow it to age.

Virginia ham (10 to 12 pounds)
2 tablespoons light brown sugar
1 tablespoon bread crumbs

1 teaspoon ground cloves
3 tablespoons honey, dry sherry, or sweet-pickle vinegar
BRANDIED PEACHES (*page 46*)

45

Preheat oven to 375° F.

Combine brown sugar, bread crumbs, and cloves and press mixture into the ham.

Place the ham in a shallow baking pan and bake at 375° F. for 15 minutes or until sugar melts.

Remove from oven and drizzle honey, sherry, or sweet-pickle vinegar on the ham.

Return to the oven for 15 minutes.

Serve garnished with Brandied Peaches, spiced crab apples, or any spiced fruit.

BRANDIED PEACHES

(*1 quart*)

Sent to family or friends back home in England, a Virginia ham made a delectable and much appreciated gift. So did peach brandy. In a letter of 1758 to Theodorick Bland, Sr., of Virginia, the Liverpool merchant Charles Gore expressed his thanks for the "kind present of hams and peach brandy."

Another favorite was brandied peaches. St. George Tucker of Williamsburg, writing to his daughter in 1804, passed on a recipe for "Brandy Peaches." * In his fine, clear handwriting he advised her:

> "Peel your peaches & put them in a stone pot—set the pot into a vessel of water, and let it boil until a straw will pierce the fruit—Then make a syrup of brandy and sugar—1 lb. of sugar to a qt. of brandy. Set in your peaches—They will be fit for use in a month—Brown sugar will do very well—Better without peeling SGT."

Today you can prepare brandied peaches by a quicker method and thereby provide an excellent accompaniment to Virginia Ham.

2 cans (1 pound, 13 ounces each) peach halves
1 cup granulated sugar
½ cup brandy, preferably a peach or fruit brandy
3 to 4 drops almond extract

46

* *Quoted by permission from the Tucker-Coleman Collection, Earl Gregg Swem Library, College of William and Mary in Virginia.*

Drain the peaches and reserve 1 cup of the juice.

Mix the sugar with the reserved peach juice and boil until reduced to one-half the original quantity.

Cool, measure, and stir in an equal amount of brandy, approximately ½ cup, and the almond extract.

Pour brandy syrup over peaches and serve or pack peaches in a sterilized one-quart glass jar, add the brandy syrup, and seal.

VIRGINIA HAM LOAF

(6 servings)

¾ pound VIRGINIA HAM *(page 45), cooked and ground*
¾ pound smoked ham, cooked and ground
1 cup potatoes, mashed
2 eggs, well beaten
1 medium onion, chopped

¼ cup bread crumbs
2 tablespoons milk
½ cup BARBECUE SAUCE *(page 91), divided*
salt and pepper to taste
cloves (optional)

Preheat oven to 350° F.

Grease an 8½ x 4½ x 2½-inch loaf pan or 6 individual loaf pans 4½ x 2½ x 1½-inches.

Mix hams together well and blend in mashed potatoes.

Stir in eggs, onion, bread crumbs, and milk.

Mix in 2 tablespoons Barbecue Sauce and salt and pepper to taste.

Turn into prepared pan or pans and press down to avoid air pockets.

Insert whole cloves if desired.

Spread remaining Barbecue Sauce over top.

Bake large loaf at 350° F. for 50 to 60 minutes or smaller loaves for 40 to 45 minutes.

Recipes

CASCADES PORK TENDERLOIN BROCHETTE

(4 servings)

1 pound pork tenderloin
TERIYAKI SAUCE (below)
1 large green pepper
1 jar (10 ounces) kumquats

1 jar (11 ounces) preserved
   orange sections with rind
12 chunks canned pineapple

Place pork into a shallow dish with Teriyaki Sauce and marinate overnight. Turn occasionally.

Prepare grill so that coals are light gray and hot when brochettes are ready.

Trim off all fat, and cut pork into 16 pieces 2½ inches square by ½ inch thick.

Cut the green pepper into 12 chunks.

Skewer pork, kumquats, pepper chunks, orange slices, and pineapple chunks alternately, repeating until all 4 skewers hold 4 pieces of pork (beginning and ending with pork) and 3 kumquats, pepper chunks, orange slices, and pineapple chunks each.

Place on grill 3 to 4 inches from hot coals; grill for 5 to 7 minutes.

Turn, baste with Teriyaki Sauce, and grill for an additional 5 to 7 minutes.

Continue basting and cooking for a total of 15 to 20 minutes or until pork is well done, with no pink showing, and browned on all sides.

Note: Saffron rice is an excellent accompaniment for this dish.

TERIYAKI SAUCE

¼ cup dry sherry
½ cup soy sauce
½ cup CHICKEN STOCK (page
  43), or canned chicken broth

½ cup pineapple juice
1 teaspoon fresh ginger, grated

Heat sherry to boiling point.
Add soy sauce, Chicken Stock, pineapple juice, and ginger.
Bring to a boil, remove from heat, and allow to cool to room temperature before marinating the pork.

PORK CHOPS AND SWEET POTATOES

(*4 servings*)

3 to 4 medium sweet potatoes
4 center-cut pork chops
salt and pepper to taste
all-purpose flour
2 tablespoons butter, melted
½ cup currant jelly

½ cup orange juice
1 tablespoon lemon juice
rind of 1 lemon, grated
1 teaspoon dry mustard
1 teaspoon paprika
½ teaspoon ground ginger

Preheat oven to 350° F.

Boil and slice sweet potatoes.

Salt and pepper chops, dredge in flour, and brown on both sides.

Melt butter in small saucepan. Stir in jelly, juices, and lemon rind. Add remaining ingredients, stirring to blend.

Arrange sweet potatoes and chops in shallow casserole and cover with ¾ cup of sauce.

Bake, uncovered, at 350° F. for 30 to 40 minutes, basting occasionally with remaining sauce.

BEEF STEAK AND KIDNEY PIE

(*5–6 servings*)

There are two versions of this old English favorite. Beef steak and kidney pie is made with a light, short crust; beef steak and kidney pudding with a light, suet crust. It seems that the pie was popular in the colonies and the pudding in England.

¾ pound top sirloin of beef,
   cut into 1-inch cubes
½ pound lamb, beef, or veal
   kidneys
¼ teaspoon salt
¼ teaspoon pepper
¼ teaspoon paprika
¼ cup all-purpose flour
1 medium onion, thinly sliced

2 tablespoons shortening
2 cups BEEF STOCK (*page 42*)
   or 2 cups beef bouillon
1 bay leaf
2 hard-cooked eggs
4 mushrooms, sautéed and
   sliced
1 cup PASTRY CRUST MIX
   (*page 131*)

49

Preheat oven to 450° F. ten minutes before pie is to go in.

Trim any fat or membrane from beef and kidneys. Cut kidneys into ⅛-inch-thick slices.

Place salt, pepper, paprika, and flour in a paper bag and shake to mix. Add beef, kidneys, and onion and shake until well coated.

Melt shortening in a large skillet or dutch oven, let it get very hot, and add beef, kidneys, and onions.

Cook and stir over high heat until meat is brown. Add Beef Stock and bay leaf.

Reduce heat to low, cover the skillet, and simmer 1 hour or until beef is tender.

Remove from heat and take out the bay leaf. Cool.

Place in 1½-quart baking dish and top with sliced eggs and mushrooms.

Moisten Pastry Crust Mix with ice water, roll out, and cover pie, sealing sides of casserole. Cut vents for steam to escape.

Bake for 10 to 15 minutes at 450° F., then reduce heat to 350° F. and bake for an additional 15 to 20 minutes or until crust is golden brown.

GINGER BEEF

(4 servings)

2 onions, chopped
1 clove garlic, chopped
1½ teaspoons turmeric
4 teaspoons powdered ginger
1½ teaspoons salt
1¼ pounds flank steak or chuck
 roast, cut in strips

½ cup vegetable oil
1 cup canned tomatoes,
 drained
1 can condensed onion soup

Combine onions, garlic, turmeric, ginger, and salt with beef and let stand for 1 hour.

Heat oil in a heavy pan and sauté beef mixture.

Add tomatoes and onion soup.

Cover and simmer 1½ to 2 hours, adding water if the mixture seems too dry.

Serve with hot rice.

ZUCCHINI STUFFED WITH LAMB AND RICE
(6 servings)

3 medium zucchini squash, washed but not peeled.
1 cup ground lamb (shoulder or lamb patties)
1 small onion, finely chopped
2 tablespoons shortening

1 tablespoon parsley, chopped
2 tablespoons lemon juice
½ cup canned tomatoes, drained and chopped
1½ cups cooked rice
salt and fresh cracked pepper

Preheat oven to 375° F.

Cut the zucchini in half lengthwise. Hollow out the centers, reserving the flesh.

Brown the lamb and chopped onion in shortening. Drain on paper towels. Add the parsley, lemon juice, tomatoes, rice, and salt and pepper and mix well.

Dice the reserved zucchini, add it to the mixture, and fill the zucchini boats with it.

Bake in a 375° F. oven 30 minutes.

KING'S ARMS TAVERN TENDERLOIN OF BEEF STUFFED WITH OYSTERS
(4 servings)

4 7-ounce tenderloin steaks
12 medium oysters
3 tablespoons butter, divided
salt and pepper to taste

4 slices bacon
1 teaspoon parsley, chopped, or fresh chives, snipped

Insert a sharp knife into the side of each tenderloin steak and, with a short sawing motion, make a pocket. Be careful not to puncture the other side of the steak.

Sauté oysters in 1 tablespoon butter, salt, pepper, and some of the oyster liquor only until edges begin to curl; drain.

Stuff each steak with three oysters, wrap with a slice of bacon, and secure it with a toothpick. Broil or sauté.

Heat remaining butter until light brown, add parsley or chives, and pour over cooked steaks.

Note: If the steaks are being prepared in advance, drain and cool the oysters before stuffing them.

51

LAMB OR VEAL CHOPS ALDEN

(*4 servings*)

4 loin lamb or veal chops
salt to taste
1 teaspoon black pepper,
   freshly ground
4 tablespoons butter, divided
8 ounces mushrooms, sliced

4 tablespoons onion, minced
2 cups ketchup
4 teaspoons currant jelly
4 tablespoons Madeira or dry
   sherry

Trim the fat off the chops and season with salt and pepper.

Melt 2 tablespoons butter in black iron skillet or dutch oven and sauté mushrooms for 3 or 4 minutes, stirring constantly. Remove and hold.

Brown chops, turning once. Hold.

Melt remaining butter in skillet and sauté onion.

Add ketchup, currant jelly, and Madeira or sherry.

Bring to a boil, reduce heat, and simmer 30 minutes.

Add browned chops and simmer 1 hour, partially covered, or until meat is tender and sauce thick and dark. Baste occasionally.

Add mushrooms 10 minutes before chops are done.

VEAL BIRDS GARNISHED WITH FRESH MUSHROOMS AND ARTICHOKE BOTTOMS

(*6 servings*)

6 veal cutlets (6 ounces each),
   well-trimmed
2 cups onions, finely diced
1 cup butter, divided
2 cups bread crumbs
½ cup seedless raisins
salt and pepper to taste
pinch powdered thyme
¼ cup milk

¼ cup all-purpose flour
½ cup dry sherry
2 cups BASIC BROWN SAUCE
   (page 92)
1 pound fresh mushrooms,
   quartered
8 artichoke bottoms, quartered
¼ cup parsley, chopped

Cut veal cutlets in half, place between layers of wax paper, one at a time, and pound thin with a mallet or the side of a heavy knife blade or cleaver.

Sauté onion in ½ cup butter, stirring so it does not brown.

Add bread crumbs, raisins, salt, pepper, and thyme.

Remove from heat, add milk, and mix well.

Spoon 2 tablespoons of mixture close to one edge of each flattened piece of veal, roll up, and fasten with a toothpick.

Season meat with salt and pepper, roll lightly in flour, and sauté in ¼ cup butter.

When brown, remove veal from pan, drain fat, add sherry, and allow to boil a second or two.

Stir in Brown Sauce, return meat to pan, and simmer over low heat, covered, for 20 to 30 minutes or until veal is tender when pierced with a fork.

Sauté mushrooms and artichokes in remaining butter.

Place veal birds on heated platter, cover with sauce, and garnish with mushrooms, artichokes, and parsley.

PORK BARBECUE SANDWICHES

(6 servings)

1½ pounds cooked pork, thinly sliced
2 cups BARBECUE SAUCE *(page 91)*

6 large hamburger rolls, warmed
dill pickle or *cole slaw*

Place pork in a shallow pan and marinate with Barbecue Sauce in a warm oven until thoroughly heated.

Spoon about 4 ounces of the pork barbecue onto each roll, and garnish with dill pickle or cole slaw.

Note: 1 heaping tablespoon of cole slaw may be placed on top of the pork barbecue in the bun.

CHRISTIANA CAMPBELL'S TAVERN
COLONIAL GAME PIE

(12–15 servings)

salt to taste
1 duck (4½ to 5 pounds)
2 pounds rabbit
2½ pounds venison
½ cup vegetable oil
2 cups port wine
1½ quarts BASIC BROWN SAUCE
   (page 92)
1 tablespoon Worcestershire
   sauce
1 clove garlic, minced
½ teaspoon black pepper,
   crushed

1 cup currant jelly
1½ pounds mushrooms,
   quartered
½ cup butter
1 pound slab bacon, cut into
   ¼-inch cubes
1 can (15½ ounces) pearl
   onions
PASTRY CRUST MIX *(page 131)*
2 eggs
¼ cup milk

Preheat oven to 400° F.

Salt cavity of duck and place on rack in shallow roasting pan, breast side up.

Bake 30 minutes at 400° F., reduce heat to 325° F., and bake until duck tests done.

Simmer rabbit in a small amount of water for 60 minutes or until tender.

Cut the venison in large cubes and sauté in the vegetable oil in a large skillet until well browned, stirring and turning as necessary.

Remove venison and drain oil from the pan.

Add port wine to the pan and boil for 2 to 3 minutes, scraping up any brown particles.

Return venison to pan and add Brown Sauce. Simmer for 45 to 60 minutes, or until venison is tender.

Cut the duck and rabbit in medium-sized pieces, and place in the pan with the venison to keep warm.

Season with Worcestershire sauce, garlic, pepper, and currant jelly.

Sauté the mushrooms in butter until lightly browned.

Fry bacon until crisp; drain.

Heat onions and drain.

Divide mixture into individual casserole dishes and garnish the top of each with mushrooms, bacon, and onions.

Cover with pastry crust, trim edges, and prick tops to allow steam to escape.

Beat eggs lightly with milk to make an egg wash and brush the tops of the pastry with the mixture.

Bake in 350° F. oven 20 to 25 minutes or until crust is golden brown.

Serve piping hot.

Poultry

R estaurateurs know that chicken, prepared one way or another, is the second most-ordered food. Chicken has held its place as first choice among poultry and wild fowl the centuries and the years around. Turkeys are traditionally reserved for special occasions.

An astonishing thing to Virginia's first settlers was the "infinities of wild Turkeyes" at large in the woods. Discovered by the Spaniards and introduced into Europe years earlier, the big bird was already domesticated and playing its part in England's Christmas fare a quarter of a century before Jamestown was founded. Housewives found that each wild bird had a finger's thickness of fat on its back, which was better and sweeter for cakemaking than the best butter. Today, game wardens seeking to restock the wild turkey for the benefit of hunters are faced with the problem of keeping the wild birds wild. They prefer the comforts of being tame.

A pair of Roast Duck with Fruit Stuffing ▶
is displayed in the dining room of the Brush-
Everard House, the platter garnished with
orange wedges, fresh mushrooms, roast pota-
toes, and seedless grapes.

WILLIAMSBURG INN
BREAST OF TURKEY SUPREME

(*6 servings*)

Brillat-Savarin (1755–1826), a famous French gastronome, said in his book on the art of dining that the turkey is surely one of the noblest gifts that the Old World received from the New. Perhaps he remembered the day during his stay in America that he killed a wild turkey in Connecticut and afterwards prepared it with his own hands. However that may be, Chef Fred Crawford of the Williamsburg Inn considered this version of Breast of Turkey Supreme, his own, to be one of his finest entrées.

½ *cup butter*
½ *cup all-purpose flour*
2 *cups hot* CHICKEN STOCK
   (*page 43*), or *canned*
   chicken broth
1 *teaspoon salt*
⅛ *teaspoon white pepper*

1 *cup milk*
1 *cup light cream*
1 *pound turkey breast, sliced*
cooked rice or *noodles*
3 *tablespoons toasted almonds,*
   chopped

Melt butter and add flour, stirring until smooth.

Pour hot Chicken Stock into butter-flour mixture and stir until smooth.

Add salt and pepper.

Heat milk and cream in a separate saucepan.

Pour into thickened Chicken Stock and cook over low heat for 10 minutes, stirring often.

Serve sauce very hot over sliced turkey breast and steamed noodles or rice.

Top with toasted almonds.

◄ *Seafood from the Chesapeake Bay is a specialty of Christiana Campbell's Tavern, one of George Washington's favorite places to dine when the House of Burgesses was in session. Arrayed here, with lobster on the sideboard, are (front row) Cascades Baked Stuffed Flounder, Christiana Campbell's Tavern Made Dish of Shrimp and Lobster, (second row) Hampton Crab Imperial, and Williamsburg Inn Corn Meal Batter Cakes with Crabmeat and Virginia Ham.*

BAKED CHICKEN WITH ALMONDS

(4 servings)

1 broiler-fryer (2¾ pound)	*½ cup blanched almonds, sliced*
all-purpose flour	*salt and pepper to taste*
½ cup butter, divided	*¼ cup dry sherry*
2 cups CHICKEN STOCK *(page 43), or canned chicken broth*	

Preheat oven to 400° F.

Cut broiler-fryer into four portions, dredge with flour, and place on rack in shallow roasting pan.

Brush with ¼ cup melted butter and bake at 400° F. until browned, 25 to 35 minutes.

When chicken is brown, remove rack, place chicken in bottom of pan and add Chicken Stock to depth of ½ inch.

Cover and bake at 350° F. for 1 hour.

Meanwhile, sauté almonds in remaining ¼ cup butter until golden brown.

About 10 minutes before the end of cooking time, remove cover and spoon almonds and butter over chicken. Season with salt and pepper.

Just before serving, sprinkle with sherry.

BONELESS BREAST OF CHICKEN

(4 servings)

4 whole chicken breasts, boned	*½ cup butter, divided*
10 large fresh mushrooms, chopped or 1 can (8 ounces) mushroom stems and pieces, drained and chopped	*salt and white pepper to taste* *drippings from chicken* CHICKEN STOCK *(page 43) or milk*
1 tablespoon shallots, finely chopped	*4 tablespoons all-purpose flour* *½ cup light cream*

Preheat oven to 375° F.

Line a shallow baking pan with foil and grease well.

Flatten chicken breasts slightly.

Sauté mushrooms and shallots in ¼ cup butter over medium heat for 5 minutes. Stir constantly.

Salt and pepper to taste.

Stuff chicken breasts with mixture and fasten securely with wooden toothpicks.

Place in prepared pan, and bake at 375° F. for 40 minutes.

Reduce heat to 350° F. and baste chicken occasionally if it seems to be browning too rapidly; bake an additional 10 to 15 minutes or until chicken is done.

Pour chicken drippings into a measuring cup and add Chicken Stock or milk to make 1 cup.

Make sauce by melting remaining butter and stirring in the flour. Remove from heat and stir in the cup of chicken drippings and the cream.

Stir until sauce is smooth, return to heat, and cook 3 to 4 minutes, stirring constantly.

Serve over chicken while hot.

CHICKEN VALENCIA
WITH RAISIN STUFFING

(6 servings)

6 large chicken breasts, boned
RAISIN STUFFING (*page 60*)
2 tablespoons all-purpose flour
1 teaspoon paprika
½ teaspoon garlic salt
Shortening for frying
½ cup orange juice
1 cup CHICKEN STOCK (*page 43*), or canned chicken broth

1 tablespoon onion, minced
salt and pepper to taste
3-inch cinnamon stick
½ cup seedless raisins
1 tablespoon sherry
1 tablespoon parsley, chopped
Orange slices

Lay chicken breasts skin side down. Place Raisin Stuffing in center of each, folding chicken over to enclose. Fasten with skewers or toothpicks.

Coat with flour mixed with paprika and garlic salt. Brown in hot shortening. Drain off fat.

Add orange juice, Chicken Stock, onion, salt and pepper to taste, and cinnamon stick. Cover.

Simmer 30 to 40 minutes until chicken is tender.

Discard cinnamon stick and skim fat from sauce. Add raisins, sherry, and parsley; simmer 3 or 4 minutes longer.

The pan sauce may be thickened slightly with a little corn-starch mixed with cold water.

Garnish with orange slices.

RAISIN STUFFING

½ cup seedless raisins, chopped
1 tablespoon sherry
1 tablespoon parsley, chopped
2 tablespoons butter, softened

2 tablespoons bread crumbs
¼ cup cooked ham, chopped
¼ teaspoon orange peel, grated

Combine all ingredients.

CHICKEN MAYONNAISE

(10–12 servings)

2 broiler-fryers (2 to 2½ pounds each)
1 onion
5 ribs of celery, divided
1 envelope unflavored gelatin
2 tablespoons lemon juice
salt and pepper to taste
¼ teaspoon leaf thyme

1 cup canned peas, drained
1½ cups mayonnaise
½ cup pecans, coarsely chopped
3 hard-cooked eggs, chopped
½ cup stuffed olives, sliced
salad greens
¼ green pepper cut in strips
1 pimiento pod

Grease a 10 x 13-inch pan.

Simmer chicken, onion and 1 rib of celery, chopped, in 1 quart water until chicken is done, about 2 hours.

Remove chicken from broth, discard skin and bones, and cut chicken into bite-sized pieces when cold.

Strain stock. Sprinkle gelatin over 1½ cups of the stock to soften, then place over low heat, stirring until dissolved; cool.

Add lemon juice, salt, pepper, and thyme.

When partially set, add 4 ribs of celery, chopped, chicken, peas, mayonnaise, pecans, eggs, and olives.

Turn into prepared pan and chill several hours until set, or overnight.

Run knife around edge and turn out onto a chilled platter or tray lined with salad greens.

Decorate with "tulips" made of green pepper and pimiento.

ROAST VIRGINIA QUAIL WITH GRAPE SAUCE AND PEACH GARNISH

(4 servings)

4 quail
6 tablespoons butter
salt and fresh cracked pepper
36 white seedless grapes, divided
4 strips salt pork, blanched
4 shallots, finely chopped
2 tablespoons cognac
1 tablespoon vegetable oil

¼ cup dry sherry
1 cup CHICKEN STOCK (page 43), or canned chicken broth
1 ½ teaspoons cornstarch
1 teaspoon lemon rind, grated
2 teaspoons lemon juice
4 peach halves, canned
guava jelly

Preheat oven to 400° F.

Salt and pepper each cavity and stuff with ½ tablespoon butter and 3 grapes.

Dry the outside of each breast with a paper towel, butter, tie with strip of salt pork, and season with salt and pepper.

Place the quail on a rack in a shallow roasting pan over the shallots and sprinkle with cognac.

Bake at 400° F. for 15 to 20 minutes, basting with 3 tablespoons butter and 1 tablespoon vegetable oil. Test for doneness.

When almost done, remove salt pork, baste, and brown under broiler. Remove to heated serving platter.

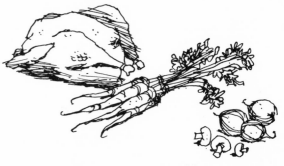

Heat remaining grapes in sherry and Chicken Stock. Remove grapes, reserve.

Add cornstarch to sherry and stock mixture, stir in grated lemon rind and lemon juice, and add to pan juices and shallots.

Stir well, scraping up brown bits on bottom, and simmer until slightly thickened.

Remove from heat, add grapes, and pour sauce over quail.

Serve immediately, garnishing each quail with a peach half filled with guava jelly.

KING'S ARMS TAVERN
CHICKEN POT PIE

(6–8 servings)

2 broiler-fryers (2½ to 3 pounds each)	*4 ribs of celery, diced and cooked*
2 ribs of celery, chopped	*4 carrots, sliced and cooked*
1 medium onion, sliced	*1¾ cups potatoes, diced and cooked*
1 bay leaf	
1 teaspoon salt	*1 egg*
½ teaspoon white pepper	*2 tablespoons milk*
½ cup butter	PASTRY CRUST MIX *(page 131),*
½ cup all-purpose flour	*as needed*
1 package (10 ounces) frozen peas, cooked	

Preheat oven to 375° F. 10 minutes before the pies are to go in the oven.

Put chicken on to cook in a large saucepan with enough water to cover.

Add 2 ribs of celery, chopped, the onion, bay leaf, salt, and pepper.

62

Bring water to a boil, reduce to a simmer and cook until chicken is done.

Remove fat and strain stock.

Discard skin and bones and cut chicken into large pieces.

Melt butter and stir in flour.

Cook 5 minutes, stirring constantly. Add enough chicken stock, stirring constantly, to achieve sauce consistency desired.

Simmer 5 minutes. Salt and pepper to taste.

Divide chicken and cooked vegetables equally into 6 or 8 individual casseroles.

Add sauce to amount desired, gently lifting chicken and vegetables so that sauce will flow down and around.

Mix egg and milk together to make egg wash.

Cover each casserole with pastry, brush with egg wash, and puncture pastry with a fork in several places to allow steam to escape.

Bake at 375° F. until crust is golden brown. Serve piping hot.

WILLIAMSBURG INN
CHICKEN AND DUMPLINGS

(6–8 servings)

*1 stewing chicken (4 to 5
    pounds) or 2 broiler-fryers
    (3 pounds each)
1 small onion, sliced
1 carrot, sliced
2 ribs of celery with leaves
1 teaspoon salt
4 tablespoons butter or chicken
    fat*

*6 tablespoons flour
⅛ teaspoon paprika
½ cup light cream
white pepper to taste*
Dumplings (*page 64*)

Simmer chicken, onion, carrot, celery, and salt in enough water to cover until chicken is done, 1½ to 2 hours.

Remove chicken from broth. When cool enough to handle, remove skin and bones, and dice meat.

63

Strain stock and, if necessary, add enough water to make 1 quart.

Melt butter or chicken fat in heavy-bottomed saucepan.

Stir in flour mixed with paprika.

Add chicken stock gradually, stirring constantly; cook for 2 minutes.

Add cream, pepper, and adjust seasoning to taste.

Spoon Dumplings on top of gently bubbling chicken mixture and cover. Cook for 15 minutes without lifting the lid.

Serve at once.

DUMPLINGS

2 cups all-purpose flour   1 tablespoon shortening
1 teaspoon salt   ¾ cup milk
4 teaspoons baking powder

Sift dry ingredients three times.

Blend in shortening with pastry blender or fork.

Add milk and mix well.

Dip teaspoon into cold water then into dough, and spoon dough onto chicken mixture as instructed above.

CHICKEN SOUFFLE

(6 servings)

3 whole chicken breasts,   6 eggs, separated
  boned and halved   ¼ cup Parmesan cheese, grated
salt to taste   4 jumbo mushrooms, sliced
½ cup butter

Preheat oven to 450° F. for individual casseroles or to 375° for shallow baking dish.

Grease 6 individual casseroles or 1 shallow baking dish.

Flatten chicken breasts with cleaver or flat side of heavy knife.

Season lightly with salt.

Melt butter over medium heat and sauté chicken breasts 5 to 7 minutes on each side.

Beat egg whites until stiff and glossy but not dry.

Beat egg yolks until thick and lemon colored.

Add Parmesan cheese to egg yolks and fold into whites.

Arrange chicken breasts in prepared casseroles or baking dish.

Lay mushroom slices around chicken.

Spoon egg and cheese mixture over chicken, bringing it out to edges as with a meringue.

Bake individual casseroles at 450° F. for 8 to 10 minutes. Bake the large dish at 375° for 15 to 20 minutes or until puffed and brown.

Serve immediately.

ROAST DUCK WITH FRUIT STUFFING

(4–6 servings)

The chances are that the roast duck on the menu nowadays is a domesticated bird. Duck hunters remember that the wild bird was the inspiration for a unique American folk art, the art of the decoy, which was first practiced by the Indian. Duck hunters also know that the canvasback is acknowledged superior in flavor to any other species of wild duck. Apparently the Indian thought so too.

Adele Earnest in *The Art of the Decoy* tells how archaeologists discovered the first known American Indian decoys, and noted that several were made out of native bulrushes and painted. The broad white saddle of feathers bound to the body, the wedge-shaped head, and the red sienna of head and neck, made them instantly recognizable as canvasback duck.

1 duck (5 to 6 pounds)   *seedless grapes*
salt and pepper to taste   *orange wedges*
FRUIT STUFFING *(page 66)*   *mushrooms*
½ cup orange juice   *roasted potatoes*

Preheat oven to 400° F.

Grease muffin tins for stuffing.

Salt and pepper inside of the duck and stuff lightly with Fruit Stuffing.

Place duck, breast up on a rack in roasting pan and bake at 400° F. for 30 minutes.

Reduce heat to 325° F. and bake until duck tests done, brushing frequently with orange juice.

Place remaining stuffing in prepared muffin tins and bake for the last 30 minutes of the baking time.

If duck browns too rapidly cover with tent of aluminum foil.

If duck appears to be fat, prick skin with fork occasionally during baking.

Duck tests done when juices are no longer pink or drumstick feels soft when pressed.

Duck is customarily served quartered or with half of a breast filet and a drumstick or thigh to each person.

Garnish with seedless grapes, orange wedges, mushrooms, and roasted potatoes.

FRUIT STUFFING

¼ cup butter
1 package (8 ounces)
  herb-seasoned dressing
1 tablespoon orange rind,
  grated

¼ cup seedless raisins or
  currants
1 large apple, grated with skin
  on

Heat butter and 1 cup water in skillet.

Stir in remaining ingredients and toss lightly.

66

Fish and Seafood

Water, and fish, are everywhere in tidewater Virginia. Besides the Atlantic Ocean and Chesapeake Bay, four great rivers reaching far inland, plus tributary rivers, creeks, and deep-water inlets, make the area a maze of waterways.

Fish, both fresh and salt water, and shellfish abound. At one time oysters existed in such incredible quantities that ships had to avoid whole banks of them; sturgeon attained a length of from nine to twelve feet. Those people who lived along a riverbank could spear fish at their door and scrape up shellfish by the bushel.

Angling is an art on which Englishmen—and Virginians—have always prided themselves. But as Robert Beverley, the first native Virginian to publish a history of the colony and an avid angler, had to admit, catching fish was hardly an art in Virginia: "I have set in the shade, at the Heads of the Rivers Angling, and spent as much time in taking the Fish off the Hook, as in waiting for their taking it."

Recipes

CHOWNING'S TAVERN
SAUTEED BACKFIN CRABMEAT

(4 servings)

1 pound backfin crabmeat
1 teaspoon lemon juice
1 tablespoon shallots, finely
  chopped

6 tablespoons butter
salt and pepper to taste
dash dry sherry or brandy

Pick over crabmeat and discard any bits of shell or cartilage.
Sprinkle with lemon juice and toss lightly.
Sauté shallots in butter over low heat until golden.
Add crabmeat and cook over low heat only until crabmeat
is hot; do not brown.
Season with salt and pepper and a dash of sherry or brandy
Serve hot in individual heated ramekins or casseroles.

CRAB CAKES

(9–12 three-inch cakes)

1 pound regular crabmeat
2 tablespoons lemon juice
Medium Cream Sauce:
  1 tablespoon butter
  1 tablespoon all-purpose
    flour
  ½ cup milk
  salt
3 eggs, divided
2 tablespoons mayonnaise

1 cup bread crumbs, divided
1 teaspoon salt
⅛ teaspoon white pepper
1 teaspoon dry mustard
2 teaspoons Worcestershire
  sauce
¼ cup milk
¼ cup all-purpose flour
1 teaspoon paprika
shortening for frying

Pick over crabmeat and discard any bits of shell or cartilage.
Sprinkle lemon juice over crabmeat.
Make a medium cream sauce by melting the butter in a
heavy skillet over medium heat and stirring in flour, milk, and
salt to taste. Continue stirring until mixture is smooth and thick.
Beat 2 eggs and add the cream sauce, mayonnaise, ¼ cup
bread crumbs, and seasonings and stir well.

68

Gently combine the crabmeat and egg mixture. Chill until firm enough to shape.

Shape into 9 to 12 three-inch patties, depending on thickness desired.

Mix remaining egg and milk together.

Bread cakes lightly by dipping into flour, beaten egg mixture, and remaining bread crumbs mixed with paprika.

Fry in ¼-inch shortening, turn once.

CRABMEAT MORNAY

(4–5 servings)

1 pound regular crabmeat
3 egg yolks
½ cup light cream
2 cups hot BÉCHAMEL SAUCE
　(page 92), divided

2 tablespoons butter
2 tablespoons whipping cream
2 tablespoons Parmesan
　cheese, grated

Preheat oven to 400° F.

Grease 1 to 1½-quart casserole or 4 to 5 individual ones.

Pick over crabmeat and discard any bits of shell or cartilage.

Mix egg yolks with light cream.

Add Béchamel Sauce (reserving 2 tablespoons for topping), butter, salt, and crabmeat.

Turn mixture into prepared casserole or casseroles.

Combine remaining sauce with whipping cream and spread over top.

Sprinkle with Parmesan cheese.

Bake at 400° F. for 20 minutes or until lightly browned and heated through.

Note: In place of the sauce-cream topping, 4 tablespoons of mayonnaise can be substituted.

CRABMEAT RAVIGOTE

(*6 servings*)

1 pound regular crabmeat	*⅔ cup mayonnaise, divided*
¼ cup tarragon vinegar	*salt and pepper to taste*
3 tablespoons pimiento,	*cleaned crab shells or lettuce*
* chopped*	*capers*
2 tablespoons chives, chopped	*pimiento*
2 tablespoons sweet pickle	
* relish*	

Pick over crabmeat and discard any bits of shell or cartilage; marinate in vinegar 15 minutes.

Drain crabmeat and add chopped pimiento, chives, relish, ½ cup mayonnaise, salt and pepper to taste.

Divide mixture evenly into 6 cleaned crab shells or crisp lettuce cups; shape into domes.

Spread with thin coating of remaining mayonnaise.

Sprinkle well-drained capers over top and garnish with pimiento.

Serve very cold.

HAMPTON CRAB IMPERIAL

(*6 servings*)

1 pound backfin crabmeat	*1 egg yolk*
½ tablespoon pimiento,	*¼ teaspoon dry mustard*
* chopped*	*1 rounded teaspoon capers,*
½ tablespoon green pepper,	* drained*
* chopped*	*1½ teaspoons Worcestershire*
1 tablespoon butter	* sauce*
Heavy Cream Sauce:	*salt and white pepper to taste*
* 4 tablespoons butter*	*1 cup mayonnaise, divided*
* 5 tablespoons all-purpose*	*paprika*
* flour*	
* 1 cup milk*	
* ½ teaspoon salt*	

Preheat oven to 375° F. 10 minutes before crab is ready to go in.

Pick over crabmeat and discard any bits of shell or cartilage. Refrigerate.

Sauté pimiento and green pepper in butter.

Make a heavy cream sauce by melting the butter in a heavy skillet over medium heat and stirring in the flour, milk, and salt. Continue stirring until mixture is smooth and thick.

Combine sautéed vegetables, cream sauce, and other ingredients except crabmeat, mayonnaise, and paprika.

Mix in ¾ cup mayonnaise.

Fold in crabmeat very gently so lumps will not break up.

Spoon into shells or shallow baking dishes and spread remaining mayonnaise on top of each crab filling.

Bake at 375° F. for 30 to 35 minutes or until golden brown.

Sprinkle with paprika and serve at once.

WILLIAMSBURG INN
CORN MEAL BATTER CAKES
WITH CRABMEAT AND VIRGINIA HAM

(10 servings)

2½ cups milk
1 cup corn meal
1 cup butter, melted
2⅔ cups all-purpose flour
2 teaspoons baking powder
1 teaspoon baking soda
1 teaspoon salt

2 tablespoons sugar
3 eggs
VIRGINIA HAM (page 45),
thinly sliced
½ recipe CHOWNING'S TAVERN
SAUTÉED BACKFIN
CRABMEAT (page 68)

Heat milk and 2 cups water almost to boiling, add corn meal, and whip until smooth. Cool to room temperature.

Add remaining ingredients, except ham and crabmeat, and beat well with a wire whisk. Batter will be thin.

Cook on a lightly greased hot griddle, allowing ¼ cup batter for each cake. Turn once when small bubbles appear on surface.

Place a slice of Virginia Ham on each cake, and top with 1 to 2 tablespoons of the crabmeat. Serve cakes flat, or roll them as you would a crepe.

Note: Batter tends to thicken towards the last of the cakes. When this happens, add a small amount of water or milk to restore original consistency.

Also note: Additional batter cakes can be frozen between squares of waxed paper for future use.

CASCADES FRIED FLOUNDER AMANDINE

(6 servings)

2 pounds fresh flounder fillets	*3 eggs, beaten*
salt and pepper to taste	*⅔ cup milk*
2 tablespoons lemon juice	*2 cups all-purpose flour*
¾ pound saltine crackers	*½ cup vegetable oil*
¾ cup almonds, sliced	*½ cup butter*

Cut flounder into 6 portions and season with salt, pepper, and lemon juice.

Coarsely crumble the crackers and mix with the almonds.

Beat the eggs and milk together to make an egg wash.

Dredge the flounder in the flour and dip into the egg wash.

Roll in the cracker-almond mixture and pat down firmly so that the mixture will adhere.

Heat the oil and butter. Fry the fish about 5 minutes on each side or until it is golden brown and flakes easily when pricked with a fork.

Drain quickly on a paper towel and serve immediately.

A Cheese Soufflé fittingly presides over an ▶ assortment of egg and cheese dishes at the Cascades. Below it, clockwise, are Williamsburg Inn Fantasio Omelets, Eggs Hunter's Style, Chowning's Tavern Welsh Rabbit, and shad roe for a Christiana Campbell's Tavern Shad Roe Omelet.

CASCADES BAKED STUFFED FLOUNDER

(*6 servings*)

6 baby flounder, boned, or
  6 flounder fillets
SEAFOOD DRESSING (*below*)
salt and pepper to taste

3 tablespoons lemon juice
1 cup fine bread crumbs
⅓ pound butter, melted

Preheat oven to 375° F.

Grease shallow baking pan.

Stuff each fish with 4 to 6 tablespoons of Seafood Dressing, or spread the same amount of dressing over each fillet. Roll and fasten with toothpicks.

Place in prepared baking pan, and season with salt, pepper, and lemon juice.

Sprinkle bread crumbs over fish.

Melt butter and pour over fish.

Bake at 375° F. for 25 to 30 minutes or until fish flakes easily when tested with a fork.

SEAFOOD DRESSING

6 tablespoons butter
¼ cup celery, finely chopped
½ cup onion, finely chopped
¼ cup green pepper, finely
  chopped
½ pound shrimp, cooked and
  diced
1 teaspoon parsley, chopped
1 teaspoon pimiento, finely
  chopped

½ teaspoon paprika
1 teaspoon Worcestershire
  sauce
½ teaspoon seafood seasoning
salt to taste
⅛ teaspoon cayenne pepper
¼ cup dry sherry
1½ cups bread crumbs

Melt butter, add the vegetables, and sauté until tender.

◄ *Salmagundi—the eighteenth-century English name for what is now known as chef's salad—as made at Christiana Campbell's Tavern, is shown here in the kitchen of Wetherburn's Tavern, among slices of ham and ingredients fresh from the garden.*

Add all of the remaining ingredients except the bread crumbs to the vegetables and cook over low heat for 10 minutes.

Add this mixture to the bread crumbs and mix thoroughly.

MOTOR HOUSE SEAFOOD GUMBO
(*8 servings*)

Although people in other countries eat okra, gumbo is distinctively American. Originally a Louisiana concoction of seafood thickened and flavored with the young and tender pods of okra and with gumbo filé powder—powdered sassafras leaves—the dish spread over the South. "Gumbo" is the Negro expression for the okra plant, which grows prolifically in the South, and may be seen in the Wythe House garden in Williamsburg. By the early 1800s a Virginia hostess spoke of gumbo as "traditional" when she was a girl. By then, too, the choice of ingredients was wider: fowl or a knuckle of veal might have been used instead of fish.

1 pound medium shrimp, raw	*dash Tabasco sauce*
celery tops	*½ teaspoon Worcestershire*
¼ cup celery, diced	*sauce*
¼ cup onion, diced	*½ bay leaf*
¼ cup green pepper, diced	*2 teaspoons salt*
1 small clove garlic, diced	*1½ teaspoons gumbo filé*
¼ cup butter, divided	*powder (see note)*
2 cups canned tomatoes	*½ cup regular crabmeat*
½ cup tomato purée	*½ cup whole oysters*
3 tablespoons all-purpose flour	*1 cup rice, cooked (optional)*
½ cup scallops, quartered	
½ cup okra, chopped (see note)	

Peel shrimp, saving hulls.

Put the shrimp hulls and a few celery tops into 2 quarts water and boil for 30 minutes; strain.

Sauté celery, onions, green pepper, and garlic in 2 tablespoons of the butter until tender but not brown.

Add tomatoes, tomato purée, and one quart of the strained stock to the sautéed vegetables.

74

Let simmer for 25 minutes.

Make a roux by melting 2 tablespoons of the butter and stirring in the flour. Mix thoroughly and cook 3 or 4 minutes but do not brown.

Stir roux into stock and cook for 5 minutes.

Add diced shrimp, scallops, okra, Tabasco sauce, Worcestershire sauce, bay leaf, and salt to stock and simmer for 20 minutes. Remove bay leaf.

Remove from the pot ½ cup of liquid, sprinkle filé powder over it, and beat until smooth.

Add to stock and simmer 5 minutes. *Be careful not to let the stock boil after the filé powder has been added or it will become stringy and unfit to serve.*

Remove from heat and add crabmeat and oysters.

Serve on plates or in casserole with or without rice.

Note: If canned okra is used, the liquid may be added to the gumbo after the cooking process as it will enhance the flavor of the soup. If raw okra is used, blanch it in 2 cups of the stock before adding with the seafood and seasonings.

Also note: Okra will take the place of filé powder if the latter is not available; however, gumbo tastes better when both okra and filé powder are used.

CHRISTIANA CAMPBELL'S TAVERN MADE DISH OF SHRIMP AND LOBSTER

(4–6 servings)

1½ green peppers, quartered
3 medium tomatoes
2 packages (6 ounces each) long grain and wild rice, mixed
½ pound fresh mushrooms, quartered
¼ pound butter, divided
¾ pound lobster, cooked and shelled

1 pound shrimp, cooked and cleaned
1 can (15½ ounces) pearl onions
¾ cup dry sherry
1 teaspoon lemon juice
Worcestershire sauce to taste
salt and white pepper to taste
parsley

Partially cook green pepper in boiling water, remove, and cut quarters in half. Reserve.

Scald tomatoes in boiling water for 60 seconds, drain, remove skin, and cut in half. Squeeze out and discard the tomato juice and cut each half into 4 pieces. Reserve.

Cook the rice according to package instructions.

Sauté mushrooms quickly in a small amount of butter and reserve.

Cut the lobster into bite-size pieces.

Melt remaining butter over medium heat and sauté lobster, shrimp, and onions.

Add sherry, lemon juice, and seasonings.

Add green pepper, tomato, and mushrooms and cook over low heat, stirring gently, until heated through.

Arrange the seafood and vegetables in a heated serving dish with the rice. Sprinkle with a dash of sherry.

Garnish with chopped parsley if desired.

TRAVIS HOUSE OYSTERS

(*6–8 servings*)

Built in 1765, the Travis House was moved to the present site of the John Greenhow House and restored in 1930. From 1931 until 1951, Colonial Williamsburg operated a restaurant there. One of its specialties was this recipe developed by the cook, Mrs. Lena Richards. After being served Travis House Oysters one admirer wrote, "The oysters—ah yes the oysters—they want nothing they have everything."

½ cup butter
½ cup all-purpose flour
1½ teaspoons paprika
½ teaspoon salt
¼ teaspoon pepper
dash cayenne
½ clove garlic, minced
1 medium onion, chopped

½ medium green pepper, chopped
1 quart fresh oysters
1 tablespoon lemon juice
2 teaspoons Worcestershire sauce
¼ cup cracker crumbs

Preheat oven to 400° F.

Grease a 2-quart casserole or 6 to 8 individual casseroles.

Melt butter in a large skillet over medium heat.

Remove from heat, add flour, and stir until smooth.

Return to heat and cook, stirring constantly, for 5 minutes or until light brown.

Add paprika, salt, pepper, cayenne, garlic, onion, and green pepper.

Cook 3 to 5 minutes, stirring constantly.

Add oysters and their liquor, lemon juice, and Worcestershire sauce. Stir well.

Pour into prepared casserole or casseroles.

Sprinkle with cracker crumbs.

Bake at 400° F. for 20 minutes.

POACHED SALMON
WITH CUCUMBER MAYONNAISE

(4–6 servings)

1 fresh salmon (4 pounds), boned and skinned
4 bay leaves
1 lemon, sliced
4 ribs of celery, chopped

1 large onion, sliced
2 drops vegetable oil
1 teaspoon salt
¼ teaspoon pepper
CUCUMBER MAYONNAISE
(page 78)

Cut salmon into individual portions.

Pour about 2 quarts of water into a roasting pan large enough to hold the salmon. Add bay leaves, lemon, celery, onion, oil, salt, and pepper and bring to a boil.

Add the salmon, reduce heat to simmer, and poach salmon about 20 minutes or until fish flakes easily when pierced with a fork.

Cool salmon in stock.

Remove and drain on paper toweling, then place in refrigerator until cold.

Serve with Cucumber Mayonnaise.

CUCUMBER MAYONNAISE

1 cup mayonnaise or ½ cup
mayonnaise and ½ cup sour
cream
3 tablespoons lemon juice
dash Tabasco sauce

¼ teaspoon curry powder
(optional)
½ cup cucumber, finely
chopped

Blend all ingredients except cucumber.
Drain the cucumber and combine with mayonnaise mixture.
Chill for several hours before serving.

SEAFOOD PIE

(4 servings)

2 chicken bouillon cubes
½ pound scallops
12 oysters
½ pound firm white fish, diced
5 tablespoons butter
¼ cup onion, chopped
¼ cup celery, finely diced

4 tablespoons all-purpose flour
½ cup lobster, cooked and cut
into bite-sized pieces
¼ cup dry sherry
salt and pepper to taste
PASTRY CRUST MIX *for 10-inch*
double-crust pie (page 131)

Preheat oven to 375° F. 10 minutes before pie is ready to go in.

Dissolve chicken bouillon cubes in 2 cups hot water and bring to a boil.

Cook scallops, oysters, and fish in chicken stock for 5 minutes or until fish flakes easily when pierced with a fork.

Remove seafood and strain stock. Reserve.

Melt butter in small skillet over medium heat, and sauté onions and celery. Stir in flour, add stock; cook and stir until thickened.

Add scallops, oysters, fish, lobster, and sherry.

Season with salt and pepper. Cool.

Line a 1-quart casserole or four individual 5-inch casseroles with pastry.

Pour in seafood and top with pastry. Cut vents in top so that steam can escape.

Bake at 375° F. for 25 to 30 minutes or until pastry is golden brown.

Eggs and Cheese

H ens' eggs are best eggs, and the best be those that be new," a fourteenth-century cookbook advised. Of which no more need be said. Of cheese much more.

Anglo-Saxon cheeses are sturdy, set firmly, and keep a long time. French and Italian cheeses are, on the whole, more expressive. Since the native cheese is usually the perfect complement to the native drink, it follows that Anglo-Saxons like cider or beer with their country cheeses; the French and the Italians drink wine with theirs. William Byrd II of Virginia liked his bread and cheese with punch.

BASIC OMELET

(2 servings)

3 eggs
1 tablespoon light cream
salt and pepper to taste

1 teaspoon butter
1 teaspoon vegetable oil

Beat eggs and cream together until mixture is light and foamy.

Salt and pepper to taste.

Heat butter and oil in an omelet pan over high heat; remove pan from heat.

Add eggs and return to heat.

When eggs begin to set, lift edges with fork or spatula so that uncooked egg will run to bottom of pan.

Shake the pan occasionally to prevent sticking.

When egg mixture is completely set, roll omelet onto warm plate and serve at once.

WILLIAMSBURG LODGE
COUNTRY OMELET

(2–3 servings)

2 teaspoons butter, divided
1 teaspoon green pepper,
   finely chopped
1 teaspoon onion, finely
   chopped

5 chicken livers
3 eggs
1 tablespoon light cream
1 teaspoon vegetable oil
salt and pepper to taste

Melt 1 teaspoon butter over medium heat in omelet pan; add green pepper and onion.

Cook, stirring, until onions are transparent; remove.

Sauté chicken livers, then chop coarsely.

Beat eggs and cream together until mixture is light and foamy.

Salt and pepper to taste.

Heat remaining butter and oil in the omelet pan over high heat; remove pan from heat.

Add eggs and return to heat.

Before eggs begin to set, add green pepper and onion.

When eggs begin to set, lift edges with fork or spatula so that uncooked egg will run to bottom of pan.

Shake the pan occasionally to prevent sticking.

When egg mixture is completely set, add chicken livers, salt, and pepper.

Fold the omelet over, roll onto warm plate, and serve at once.

CHRISTIANA CAMPBELL'S TAVERN SHAD ROE OMELET

(1–2 servings)

3 ounces shad roe	*¼ cup light cream*
salt and pepper to taste	*¼ cup fine bread crumbs*
2 eggs	*2 tablespoons butter*

Drop shad roe into boiling salted water and cook until roe is firm (about 6 minutes).

Remove from water, chop coarsely, and season with salt and pepper.

Beat eggs, cream, and bread crumbs together until mixture is light and foamy.

Salt and pepper to taste.

Heat butter in an omelet pan over high heat; remove pan from heat.

Add eggs and return to heat.

When eggs begin to set, lift edges with fork or spatula so that uncooked egg will run to bottom of pan.

Shake the pan occasionally to prevent sticking.

When egg mixture is completely set, add shad roe, fold omelet over, roll onto warm plate, and serve at once.

WILLIAMSBURG INN FANTASIO OMELET

(2–3 servings)

1 medium apple	*3 eggs*
1 slice stale bread	*1 tablespoon light cream*
¼ cup butter, divided	*¼ cup Cheddar cheese,*
2 ounces sausage meat	*shredded*
1 teaspoon chopped walnuts	
or pecans	

Peel and dice apple.

Trim slice of bread and cut into croutons. Fry until brown and crisp in 1 tablespoon butter, turning to brown on all sides; reserve.

Crumble sausage meat and cook; drain and reserve.

Sauté apple in sausage drippings and, when almost done, add chopped walnuts or pecans.

Combine croutons, sausage, apple, and nuts; hold.

Beat eggs and cream together until mixture is light and foamy.

Salt and pepper to taste.

Heat remaining butter in an omelet pan over high heat; remove pan from heat.

Add eggs and return to heat.

When eggs begin to set, lift edges with fork or spatula so that uncooked eggs will run to bottom of pan.

Shake the pan occasionally to prevent sticking.

When eggs are completely set, mound apple mixture and the shredded cheese on half the omelet; fold and roll onto warm plate and serve at once.

EGGS IN CHEESE SAUCE

(4–6 servings)

CHEESE SAUCE *(page 93)*	*paprika*
6 hard-cooked eggs, sliced	*chopped parsley*
buttered toast	

82

Prepare the Cheese Sauce.

Gently stir sliced eggs into the hot sauce.

When eggs are hot, spoon mixture over hot toast.

Garnish with a sprinkle of paprika and chopped parsley if desired.

EGGS HUNTER'S STYLE

(2 servings)

1 tablespoon onion, chopped
3 tablespoons olive oil or
    butter
4 chicken livers, quartered
1 tablespoon tomato paste

¼ cup dry white wine
4 eggs
salt and pepper to taste
buttered toast

Sauté onion in oil or butter for 5 minutes or until golden.

Add chicken livers, cooking and stirring 3 or 4 minutes.

Blend tomato paste with 4 tablespoons warm water, stir into chicken livers and onions, and simmer 5 minutes.

Add wine and cook 3 minutes, stirring occasionally.

Break eggs into sauce, being careful not to break yolks.

Cover pan and cook over medium heat 3 minutes or until whites are firm.

Season to taste, serve on rounds of buttered toast, and garnish with tomato quarters and parsley.

BAKED EGGS IN CASSEROLE

(4 servings)

5 ounces VIRGINIA HAM (page
    45), thinly sliced
6 hard-cooked eggs, sliced
salt to taste
1½ cups BÉCHAMEL SAUCE
    (page 92)

2 tablespoons bread crumbs
½ cup Swiss cheese, grated
dash of paprika

Preheat oven to 375° F.

Cut ham into thin strips, and arrange a layer of ham, then eggs, in 4 individual ramekins or in a 1½-quart casserole.

Salt the eggs to taste and top with Béchamel Sauce.

Sprinkle lightly with bread crumbs, Swiss cheese, and paprika.

Bake at 375° F. for 8 to 10 minutes for the individual ramekins and 12 to 15 minutes for the 1½-quart casserole, or until cheese is bubbly and golden brown.

CHEESE SOUFFLE

(*4–6 servings*)

½ cup butter
½ cup all-purpose flour
2 cups milk
½ teaspoon salt
dash of Tabasco sauce or
   cayenne pepper

2 cups sharp Cheddar cheese,
   grated
6 eggs, separated
1½ teaspoons dry mustard

Preheat oven to 375° F.

Grease a 2-quart soufflé dish. If an especially high soufflé is desired, tie a 2-inch collar of well-buttered paper around the top of the dish.

Melt butter over medium heat in a double-boiler or heavy-bottomed saucepan.

Stir in flour and cook for a minute, then gradually add milk, stirring constantly until mixture is smooth and thickened.

Add salt and Tabasco sauce or cayenne pepper.

Remove from heat, add cheese and stir until cheese is melted, returning to heat if necessary.

Beat egg yolks until light and add, stirring constantly.

Add mustard and allow to cool completely.

Beat egg whites until they hold soft peaks, then gently fold cheese mixture into egg whites.

Pour into prepared dish and bake at 375° F. for 15 minutes, then reduce heat to 300° F. and continue baking for 40 to 50 minutes.

Serve at once with a bit of the crust for each person.

CHOWNING'S TAVERN
WELSH RABBIT WITH BEER

(4 servings)

Welsh rabbit, or rarebit, has nothing to do with rabbit, but it is indeed a rare bit. There are quite different versions of its origin. Though Welsh by name, the "rabbit" is traditionally Old English, made from Cheddar or a Cheddar-type cheese produced for centuries at Cheddar in the English West Country, quite a step away from the Welsh border.

In 1774 Mrs. Hannah Glasse, in her *Art of Cookery Made Plain and Easy*, advised: "Toast the Bread on both Sides, then toast the Cheese on one Side, lay it on the Toast, and with a hot Iron brown the other Side." Another English cookbook makes this instruction clearer: Once the cheese is poured over the hot buttered toast, "hold the red-hot fire shovel over it."

Welsh rabbit is a favorite snack at Chowning's Tavern, and beer is its proper accompaniment.

1 tablespoon butter
1 pound sharp Cheddar
  cheese, grated
¾ cup beer, divided
dash of cayenne pepper or
  Tabasco sauce

1 teaspoon dry mustard
½ teaspoon salt
½ teaspoon Worcestershire
  sauce
1 egg, slightly beaten

Melt butter in top part of double boiler.

Add cheese and all except 1 tablespoon of beer.

Cook over hot, not boiling water, until cheese melts.

Combine seasonings with remaining tablespoon of beer and stir into cheese.

Stir in slightly beaten egg.

Serve immediately over toast or broiled tomato halves.

Note: Any cheese mixture that is left can be refrigerated and used as an excellent spread for crackers or toast.

Salads

In Elizabethan England fresh salad was always the first dish served at the five o'clock supper. England's John Evelyn wrote a discourse on *Sallets* in 1699 and listed some seventy-three kinds of *Esculents*. He advised that the greens be washed and drained in a "Cullender," and then swung in a clean napkin. After discreet choice of a mixture of olive oil, wine vinegar, salt, and pepper, with a touch of sugar according to taste, he wrote, "Composition is perfect."

CHRISTIANA CAMPBELL'S TAVERN
SALMAGUNDI

(8 servings)

Salmagundi was eighteenth-century England's name for what today is generally known in the United States as chef's salad. In present-day England, and in Colonial Williamsburg the name has been revived. In colonial times salmagundi was served as a second course, or for supper.

salad greens (Boston, romaine, endive, water cress, and others, enough to serve 8)	*4 hard-cooked eggs, sliced*
	16 sweet gherkins
	8 celery hearts
1 pound VIRGINIA HAM *(page 45), thinly sliced and cut into strips*	*16 sardines*
	16 anchovy filets
	OIL AND VINEGAR DRESSING *(page 94)*
1 pound chicken or *turkey, thinly sliced and cut into strips*	

Arrange the greens on individual salad plates or on a large platter.

Place remaining ingredients evenly over the top and around the greens.

Sprinkle lightly with Oil and Vinegar Dressing.

WILLIAMSBURG LODGE
CRABMEAT SALAD

(4 servings)

1 pound backfin crabmeat	*few drops of Tabasco sauce*
1 cup celery, diced	*¼ teaspoon Worcestershire sauce*
⅓ cup mayonnaise	
1 tablespoon lemon juice	*2 tablespoons* FRENCH DRESSING *(page 93)*
½ teaspoon salt	
dash of white pepper	*lettuce*

87

Pick over crabmeat and discard any bits of shell or cartilage.
Combine crabmeat and celery.

Mix remaining ingredients together (except lettuce), and pour over crabmeat.

Mix gently to avoid breaking lumps of crabmeat.
Serve on lettuce.

AVOCADO SALAD RING

(*5–6 servings*)

1 envelope unflavored gelatin	*½ cup mayonnaise*
2 tablespoons lemon juice, divided	*salt and pepper to taste*
	dash cayenne or *to taste*
1 heaping cup avocado, mashed	*salad greens*
	fresh tomatoes or *fresh shrimp*
½ cup sour cream	

Lightly oil 1½-quart ring mold.

Soften gelatin in ¼ cup cold water, add 1 cup boiling water and 1 tablespoon lemon juice, and stir until dissolved.

Chill until slightly thickened.

Mash avocado and put through sieve.

Blend sour cream with mayonnaise and add to avocado alternately with remaining lemon juice.

Add seasonings to taste and combine with gelatin.

Pour into prepared ring mold and chill until firm.

Unmold onto serving dish covered with greens. Fill center with diced fresh tomatoes or fresh shrimp.

BLACK CHERRY SALAD

(*6 servings*)

2 cups canned pitted black cherries	*⅓ cup dry sherry*
	lettuce
1 package (3 ounces) black cherry flavor gelatin	FRENCH DRESSING (*page 93*)
	or WILLIAMSBURG LODGE
1 tablespoon lemon juice	HONEY DRESSING (*page 95*)

Drain cherries and reserve one cup cherry juice.

Dissolve gelatin in ½ cup boiling water.

Add lemon juice, cherry juice, and sherry.

Rinse 3-cup mold or 6 individual molds in cold water.

Pour in cherry mixture and chill until partially set.

Add cherries and return to refrigerator until firm.

Serve on lettuce with French Dressing or Williamsburg Lodge Honey Dressing.

Note: This may be served as a dessert also. Substitute sweet sherry for the dry sherry and serve with a whipped topping.

FROZEN FRUIT SALAD

(8–9 servings)

2 cups fruit cocktail
1 cup mandarin orange sections
1 package (3 ounces)
  lemon flavor gelatin
2 tablespoons lemon juice
½ cup mayonnaise

½ teaspoon salt
1 cup miniature marshmallows
½ cup whipping cream
lettuce
WILLIAMSBURG LODGE HONEY DRESSING (*page 95*)

Lightly oil 8 individual molds or an 8-inch square pan.

Drain fruit cocktail and orange sections, reserving 1 cup fruit juice.

Heat fruit juice, add gelatin, and stir until dissolved.

Add lemon juice and chill until partially set.

Fold in fruit cocktail, orange sections, mayonnaise, salt, and miniature marshmallows.

Whip cream and fold in.

Turn into prepared molds.

Freeze until firm.

Serve on lettuce with Williamsburg Lodge Honey Dressing.

Note: This may be served as a dessert also. Substitute sour cream for the mayonnaise, refrigerate until firm enough to cut instead of freezing, and serve on chilled plates.

Dressings and Sauces

As one eighteenth-century English cookbook put it, the common or everyday sauces—butter, bread, egg, celery, onion, mushroom, and white sauces as well as gravy—belong to "the Rudiments of Cookery."

Sauces, for the most part, sound misguidingly simple to make. For that reason they are all the easier to spoil. Unless the first stage in the making of a sauce is just right, nothing can make the finished product good.

Mrs. Mary Randolph, in her day reputed to be the best cook in Richmond, wrote the first printed southern cookbook *The Virginia Housewife* (1842). In prefacing her instructions for melting butter as a first step in making butter sauce she warned "Nothing is more simple than this process, and nothing so generally done badly."

There were other sauces, then as now, that accompanied certain dishes; applesauce for goose, mint sauce for lamb, and various fish sauces for fish. In Virginia, shellfish was freely used, especially the large and succulent oysters that were so abundant. Landon Carter of Sabine Hall would harvest twenty bushels at a time, some reserved "for Sauces of all kinds."

Now as then, a good sauce can make a poor dish passable, a passable one good, and beyond that the heights to which a sauce may ascend depend solely on the saucemaker's art. Saucemaking has often paved the way to culinary fame. The truly imaginative *saucier* can compound an infinity of sauces from a mere handful of foundation sauces by adding a pinch of this and a touch of that, in varying degrees.

ALMOND BUTTER SAUCE

(¾ cup)

2 tablespoons slivered almonds
½ cup butter, divided
2 tablespoons pimiento, finely
   chopped
2 teaspoons parsley, finely
   chopped
2 teaspoons lemon juice
1 teaspoon salt

Sauté almonds in 2 tablespoons butter slowly until golden brown. Cool.

Cream remaining butter and add almonds, pimiento, parsley, lemon juice, and salt; mix thoroughly.

Serve with fried or broiled seafoods.

Note: If fresh parsley is not available, 1 teaspoon dried parsley leaves can be reconstituted in the lemon juice before adding to the butter mixture.

Also note: This sauce can be stored in the refrigerator for 2 weeks.

BARBECUE SAUCE

(2½ cups)

1 cup onion, finely chopped
1 clove garlic, minced
¼ cup butter, melted
1 cup ketchup
½ cup dry sherry
1 tablespoon light brown sugar
1 teaspoon dry mustard
1 tablespoon lemon juice
½ cup white vinegar
2 teaspoons Worcestershire
   sauce

In a deep saucepan sauté onion and garlic in melted butter for 3 to 4 minutes.

Add remaining ingredients and ⅓ cup water and bring to a boil.

Lower heat and simmer, uncovered, for 1 hour, stirring frequently to prevent scorching.

Strain through a fine sieve.

BASIC BROWN SAUCE

(1½ quarts)

¼ cup butter
1 cup all-purpose flour
½ cup tomato purée
2 quarts hot BEEF STOCK
  (page 42)
1 tablespoon powdered beef
  bouillon

1 tablespoon bottled brown
  gravy sauce
salt to taste
caramel color (optional)

Melt butter in large heavy saucepan over low heat, and gradually add flour, stirring constantly, until mixture is chestnut brown. It may be necessary to turn off heat completely at intervals so that flour will not burn or become too dark.

When desired color has been reached, add tomato purée and stir well.

Gradually add hot stock and powdered beef bouillon, using wire whisk to insure smoothness.

Bring mixture to a boil, then reduce heat to lowest degree possible.

Simmer 2 hours or until sauce has been reduced to about 1½ quarts.

Add bottled brown gravy sauce, salt, and caramel color if desired.

Remove from heat and strain through a fine sieve.

Cool to room temperature and refrigerate.

BECHAMEL SAUCE

(2¼ cups)

4 tablespoons butter
1 small onion, grated
4 tablespoons all-purpose flour

2 cups hot milk or 1 cup hot
  milk and 1 cup hot CHICKEN
  STOCK (page 43)
¼ teaspoon salt

Heat butter and onion together but do not brown.

Stir in flour and remove from heat.

Add hot milk or milk and chicken stock mixture and continue to stir rapidly until sauce is smooth.

Return to heat, stirring continuously until sauce comes to a boil. Gently simmer and stir 3 to 5 minutes longer.

Strain through a fine sieve.

CHEESE SAUCE

(2 cups)

2 tablespoons butter	*dash of Worcestershire sauce*
1 teaspoon onion, finely grated	*pinch of cayenne*
2 tablespoons all-purpose flour	*½ teaspoon paprika*
1½ cups light cream	*salt to taste*
¾ cup Cheddar cheese, grated	

Melt butter over medium heat, add onion and cook only until onion is golden.

Stir in flour and add cream to make a cream sauce.

Add cheese and remaining seasonings and stir only until cheese is melted.

Note: This is excellent served as a spread, or in place of hollandaise sauce on vegetables.

FRENCH DRESSING

(1 cup)

1 teaspoon salt	*¼ cup wine vinegar*
½ teaspoon black pepper,	*6 tablespoons virgin olive oil*
* freshly ground*	*6 tablespoons vegetable oil*
¾ teaspoon dry mustard	

Mix dry ingredients in a jar. Add vinegar, cover, and allow to steep a few minutes.

Beat with a small wire whisk or fork while gradually adding oils.

Cover and use at room temperature.

GARLIC FRENCH DRESSING

(1 cup)

Follow instructions for French Dressing. (page 93).

Add garlic salt or 1 small clove of garlic, crushed, to the dry ingredients and vinegar.

ROQUEFORT FRENCH DRESSING

(1 cup)

Follow instructions for French Dressing (page 93).

After beating in the oils, add ¼ cup crumbled Roquefort cheese and ¼ teaspoon onion juice.

Shake gently to mix.

OIL AND VINEGAR DRESSING

(1 pint)

1½ teaspoons salt   *½ cup cider vinegar*
¾ teaspoon white pepper   *1½ cups vegetable oil*

Dissolve the salt and pepper in the vinegar.

Add the vegetable oil and shake vigorously in a covered jar.

WILLIAMSBURG LODGE
HONEY DRESSING

(1¾ cups)

½ cup vinegar	*1 teaspoon celery seed*
¼ cup sugar	*1 teaspoon celery salt*
¼ cup honey	*1 teaspoon onion juice*
1 teaspoon dry mustard	*1 cup vegetable oil*
1 teaspoon paprika	

Mix the vinegar, sugar, honey, mustard, and paprika together, boil 3 minutes, and cool.

Add the celery seed and salt, onion juice, and vegetable oil and beat or shake vigorously.

Serve with any fresh or frozen fruit salad.

If kept under refrigeration, shake well before using.

CASCADES PEPPER DRESSING

(1 cup)

1 cup mayonnaise	*½ teaspoon salt*
⅛ cup water	*¼ teaspoon garlic powder*
½ teaspoon lemon juice	*1 tablespoon Parmesan cheese, grated*
¼ teaspoon Worcestershire sauce	*dash of Tabasco sauce*
¼ teaspoon bottled steak sauce	*1 tablespoon fresh cracked pepper*
¼ teaspoon dry mustard	
¼ teaspoon sugar	

Blend ingredients together, whipping by hand.
Refrigerate before serving.

RUM BUTTER SAUCE

(3 cups)

1 cup sugar	*2 tablespoons brandy*
2 tablespoons cornstarch	*¼ teaspoon nutmeg*
½ cup lemon juice	*½ cup light rum*
rind of 1 lemon, grated	*2 tablespoons dark rum*
½ cup butter	

95

Blend sugar and cornstarch in 1 cup boiling water.

Cook, stirring constantly, over medium heat, until mixture begins to thicken.

Add remaining ingredients and cook 2 minutes, stirring constantly.

Serve hot over mince pie, pound cake, or puddings.

WILLIAMSBURG INN REGENCY DRESSING
(3 cups)

1 tablespoon all-purpose flour
2 cups CHICKEN STOCK *(page 43), divided*
1 tablespoon onion, finely chopped
1 clove garlic

½ cup vegetable oil, divided
2 tablespoons French-style prepared mustard
salt and pepper to taste
½ cup vinegar
1 egg yolk, lightly beaten

Mix flour thoroughly with ½ cup Chicken Stock.

Bring remaining 1½ cups Chicken Stock to a boil and stir in the flour mixture.

Cook 5 minutes over medium heat, stirring constantly; remove from heat.

Purée onion and garlic in ¼ cup vegetable oil in a blender; transfer to mixing bowl.

Add seasonings, vinegar, and egg yolk, and mix.

Add remaining oil very slowly, beating constantly.

Add hot stock while continuing to beat.

Cool to room temperature before refrigerating.

Note: This dressing goes exceptionally well with hearts of Boston lettuce, water cress or endive; or any combination of fresh vegetables.

Vegetables

During his presidency, when he had little time to garden, Thomas Jefferson kept an account showing the earliest and latest appearance of each vegetable on the Washington market. He noted thirty-seven varieties of garden produce. New varieties of beans and peas—including black-eyed peas—pumpkins and squash, sweet potatoes and yams, plus all the culinary plants that grew in England, gave early Virginians a greater variety of vegetables than any other people at that time.

Corn was the single most important vegetable for both the Indians and the colonists. Dried and ground it became meal, used in making bread. Possibly the favorite way of serving corn—then as now—was on the cob. As Virginia historian Robert Beverley described it in 1705:

> They [the Indians] delight much to feed on Roasting-ears; that is, the *Indian* corn, gathered green and milky, before it is grown to its full bigness, and roasted before the Fire, in the Ear . . . And indeed this is a very sweet and pleasing food.

CORN PUDDING

(6 servings)

3 eggs
2 cups cream style corn
1½ tablespoons sugar
½ teaspoon salt

1 cup bread crumbs
2 tablespoons butter, melted
2 cups milk
½ cup light cream

Preheat oven to 350° F.
Grease 1½ quart casserole.
Beat eggs until light and fluffy.
Stir in corn, sugar, salt, bread crumbs, and butter.
Add milk and cream and mix well.
Pour into prepared casserole and place dish in pan of boiling water.
Bake at 350° F. for 50 to 60 minutes or until custard is set.

CORN PUFFS

(12 puffs)

1 egg, separated
⅓ cup milk
1 tablespoon butter, melted
½ cup cream-style corn

1 cup sifted all-purpose flour
1½ teaspoons baking powder
1 teaspoon salt

Beat egg yolk. Add milk, butter, corn, and sifted dry ingredients.
Fold in stiffly beaten egg white.
Drop by tablespoonsful into deep hot fat and fry until brown, about 3 minutes, turning once.

BRUSSELS SPROUTS
WITH CHESTNUTS
(2–4 servings)

1 pound brussels sprouts
½ cup canned chestnuts,
  chopped

salt to taste
2 tablespoons butter

Cook brussels sprouts until tender but still firm; drain.
Sprinkle chestnuts and liquid from can over sprouts and season well.
Dot with butter.
Serve hot.

CARROT PUDDING
(10–12 servings)

The carrot is one of the very few vegetables that England can claim as truly native. An old recipe for carrot pudding gives the same ingredients as this one, except for the addition of "beaten Spice." The recipe concluded: "and so have you a Composition for any Root-Pudding."

3 eggs, separated
4 tablespoons sugar
1½ tablespoons cornstarch
1 cup milk
3 cups (2 pounds) carrots,
  cooked and mashed
3 tablespoons butter

1 teaspoon salt
1 cup fine bread crumbs
1 cup light cream
½ teaspoon fresh nutmeg,
  grated
¼ cup cream sherry

Preheat oven to 300° F.
Grease 2-quart casserole.
Beat egg yolks and sugar until light, hold.
Mix cornstarch with small amount of milk.

Heat remaining milk, add cornstarch and stir until smooth and slightly thickened.

Stir small amount of hot cornstarch mixture into egg yolks and sugar.

Stir to mix well then return to hot milk and cornstarch, cooking and stirring over medium heat until smooth and thick.

Add carrots, butter, salt, and bread crumbs; blend evenly.

Stir in cream and add nutmeg and sherry; mix well.

Beat egg whites until they hold firm peaks; fold into carrot mixture.

Pour into prepared casserole.

Place casserole in pan of hot water and bake at 300° F. for 30 minutes.

Increase heat to 350° F. and bake an additional 45 minutes or until knife inserted in center comes out clean.

SCALLOPED TOMATOES AND ARTICHOKE HEARTS

(6–8 servings)

1 can (2 pounds 3 ounces) whole plum tomatoes
1 can (14 ounces) artichoke hearts
½ cup onion, finely chopped
2 tablespoons shallots, finely chopped

¼ pound butter
½ teaspoon leaf basil
2 tablespoons sugar
salt and pepper to taste

Preheat oven to 325° F.

Grease shallow earthenware or other casserole.

Drain tomatoes and artichokes; rinse artichokes in water, and quarter.

Sauté onions and shallots in butter until tender.

Add tomatoes, artichokes, and basil; heat 2 or 3 minutes, stirring gently.

Season with sugar, salt, and pepper.

Turn into prepared casserole and bake at 325° F. for 10 to 15 minutes or until vegetables are heated through.

KING'S ARMS TAVERN
CREAMED CELERY WITH PECANS
(6 servings)

4 cups celery, cut diagonally
   in ½-inch pieces
2 tablespoons butter
2 tablespoons all-purpose flour

2 cups milk
1 teaspoon salt
¾ cup pecan halves
buttered bread crumbs

Preheat oven to 400° F.
Grease 1½-quart casserole.
Boil celery until tender in enough water to cover; drain.
Melt butter over medium heat; stir in flour and add milk slowly to make cream sauce, stirring until thick and smooth.
Add salt and well-drained celery.
Spoon into prepared casserole, top with pecans, and cover with buttered bread crumbs.
Bake at 400° F. for 15 minutes.

KING'S ARMS TAVERN
CREAMED ONIONS WITH PEANUTS
(4–5 servings)

16 whole small white onions
2 tablespoons butter
2 tablespoons all-purpose flour
¼ teaspoon salt
2 cups milk

¼ cup whole salted peanuts
½ cup buttered bread crumbs
¼ cup salted peanuts, coarsely
   chopped

Preheat oven to 400° F.
Grease 1-quart casserole.
Cook onions in boiling salted water until tender; drain.
Melt butter over medium heat; stir in flour and salt.
Add milk and cook over medium heat, stirring constantly until smooth and slightly thickened.
Put onions in prepared casserole and pour cream sauce over them.

Stir in ¼ cup whole peanuts.

Top with buttered crumbs and chopped peanuts.

Bake at 400° F. for 15 minutes or until casserole is bubbly and lightly browned.

KING'S ARMS TAVERN
SWEET POTATOES

(8–10 servings)

3 pounds sweet potatoes	½ teaspoon cinnamon
¾ cup light brown sugar, packed, divided	½ teaspoon nutmeg
	¼ teaspoon salt
3 tablespoons butter	1 cup milk

Preheat oven to 400° F.

Grease 1½-quart casserole.

Cook sweet potatoes in boiling salted water until done; peel and mash.

Stir in all of remaining ingredients except 2 tablespoons of sugar.

Turn mixture into prepared casserole and sprinkle with remaining sugar.

Bake at 400° F. for 30 minutes.

CREAMED SALSIFY OR OYSTER PLANT
(4 servings)

John Randolph of Williamsburg, the last king's attorney for the colony, wrote a *Treatise on Gardening.* It was the first kitchen garden book known to have been printed in America. In it were directions for growing "Salsify, or goat's beard, *Trapopogon.*" Randolph surely knew that the second common name was a translation from the Greek: *trogos* for goat and *pogon,* beard, and was given to the plant on account of the silky supports of the purple rayed flowerheads. Today salsify is still grown in Williamsburg for its edible roots, and is regarded as a gourmet vegetable, whether purchased fresh or put up in cans or glass jars. Because the long, tapering, white-skinned roots have a delicate oysterlike flavor, salsify is also known as oyster plant or vegetable oyster.

1 can (15 ounces) or jar
   (12½ ounces) salsify
4 tablespoons butter
1 teaspoon onion,
   finely chopped
6 sprigs of parsley,
   finely chopped

¼ cup all-purpose flour
1 cup hot milk
1 cup hot light cream
¼ teaspoon nutmeg
dash of Tabasco sauce
salt and white pepper to taste

Heat salsify; drain.
Heat butter, onion, and parsley together but do not brown.
Stir in flour and continue stirring over low heat for 3 to 5 minutes.
Add hot milk and cream and stir rapidly until sauce is smooth.
Continue to stir until sauce comes to a boil. Gently simmer and stir 3 to 5 minutes longer.
Add the nutmeg and Tabasco sauce and season to taste.
Strain through a fine sieve.
Pour cream sauce over salsify and serve hot.

SALSIFY OR OYSTER PLANT FRITTERS

(4 servings)

1 can (15 ounces) or jar	*3 tablespoons all-purpose*
(12½ ounces) salsify	*flour*
1 tablespoon parsley, chopped	*⅓ cup lukewarm water*
Marinade:	*salt*
6 tablespoons salad oil	*1 teaspoon salad oil*
3 tablespoons lemon juice	*1 egg white*

Roll pieces of salsify in parsley and put in a bowl.

Mix 6 tablespoons of the salad oil with the lemon juice, pour over the salsify, and marinate for 15 minutes. Drain well.

Combine the flour, water, a pinch of salt, and 1 teaspoon of salad oil and blend until smooth. Fold in the egg white, stiffly beaten.

Dip the pieces of salsify in the batter and fry in deep hot fat or oil (375°F.) for about 4 minutes or until they are golden brown.

Drain the fritters on paper towels, sprinkle with salt, and serve warm.

SCALLOPED TOMATOES

(4 servings)

1 small onion, chopped	*5 cups (2½ pounds)*
4 tablespoons butter	*canned tomatoes*
1½ cups dry unseasoned	*1 teaspoon salt*
bread cubes	*½ teaspoon fresh*
½ cup light brown sugar	*cracked pepper*

Preheat oven to 350° F.

Grease shallow earthenware or other casserole.

Sauté onion in butter until soft, but not brown.

Add bread cubes and brown sugar, stirring over low heat 3 to 5 minutes.

Stir in tomatoes; add seasoning.

Put tomatoes in prepared casserole and bake at 350° F. for 30 to 40 minutes or until casserole is bubbly.

Vegetables

CASCADES RATATOUILLE
(8–10 servings)

1½ pounds zucchini squash
3 ribs of celery
1 large onion
1 large green pepper
1 large eggplant
8 medium tomatoes
½ cup butter

3 cloves garlic, minced
1 tablespoon oregano
1 tablespoon basil
1 tablespoon salt
1 teaspoon pepper
4 tablespoons Parmesan
   cheese, grated

Preheat oven to 350° F.

Grease large shallow earthenware or other casserole.

Slice zucchini and celery; cut onion and green pepper into large squares; and cut eggplant into large cubes.

Scald tomatoes in boiling water for 60 seconds, drain, remove skin, and cut in half. Squeeze out and discard the tomato juice and cut each half into 4 pieces. Reserve.

Blanch until barely tender in boiling salted water the zucchini, celery, green pepper, and eggplant. Drain and reserve.

Sauté onions in butter for 4 to 5 minutes.

Add garlic, oregano, basil, salt, and pepper, and continue to sauté until onions are transparent.

Combine all ingredients in prepared casserole and sprinkle with Parmesan cheese.

Bake at 350° F. for 20 to 25 minutes or until bubbly.

ARTICHOKE BOTTOMS AU GRATIN
(3–4 servings)

1 can (15 ounces)
  artichoke bottoms
1 teaspoon Worcestershire
  sauce
⅛ teaspoon nutmeg

dash of cayenne pepper
2 cups CHEDDAR CHEESE
  SAUCE (*page 106*)
Parmesan cheese, grated

Preheat oven to 300° F.

Grease shallow earthenware or other casserole.

Drain and rinse artichoke bottoms; put in prepared casserole.

Combine seasonings with the Cheddar Cheese Sauce and pour over artichokes.

Sprinkle with Parmesan cheese and bake at 300° F. for 30 minutes or until casserole is bubbly.

Brown under broiler and serve at once.

CHEDDAR CHEESE SAUCE

(2 cups)

4 tablespoons butter
¼ cup all-purpose flour
2 cups hot milk

1 cup Cheddar cheese, grated
salt and white pepper to taste

Melt butter over medium heat.

Add flour and stir for 3 to 5 minutes.

Pour in hot milk and continue to stir rapidly until sauce is smooth.

Continue to stir until sauce comes to a boil. Gently simmer and stir 3 to 5 minutes longer.

Add cheese and stir only until it is melted.

Season to taste.

ZUCCHINI WITH WALNUTS

(4 servings)

1 cup walnuts, divided
6 medium zucchini squashes,
  cut in ½-inch pieces
2 tablespoons butter

2 tablespoons olive oil
1 teaspoon salt
½ teaspoon fresh cracked
  pepper

Chop ¾ cup of the walnuts.

Sauté zucchini in butter and olive oil until tender but not crisp, shaking the pan and tossing the zucchini with a wooden spoon so that it cooks evenly.

Pour off the butter and oil and add the chopped walnuts, salt, and pepper to the drained zucchini.

When the walnuts are well blended and heated, garnish with the remaining nuts and serve.

Breads

The Bread in Gentlemen's Houses, is generally made of Wheat, but some rather choose the Pone, which is the Bread made of *Indian* Meal . . . and so called from the Indian name *Oppone*. . . ." So wrote Robert Beverley in 1705. No bread made from wheat was held to be nearly so sustaining as that made from corn; besides, the yield of corn per acre compared to that of wheat was better than twenty to one. But wheat flour was finer than corn meal, and among the gentry buttered wheat bread and tea made a desirable snack between breakfast and early afternoon dinner. Corn bread was the bread to work and travel on. At Mount Vernon, "Indian cakes for breakfast after the Virginia fashion" was the rule.

Corn meal could be made into more kinds of bread. The three mainstays—corn pone, ashcake, and hoecake—are similar to New England's journey or johnnycake, which is meal, water, and salt mixed into a stiff dough and shaped by hand. Pone was baked as the Indians baked it, in cakes before the fire. So was ashcake, "in Loaves on a warm Hearth, covering the Loaf with Leaves, then with warm Ashes, and afterwards with Coals over all." Ashcake was a staple of Negro cabins throughout the South before the Civil War. Hoecake was simply pone cooked on the blade of a hoe in the fireplace or over an open fire in the fields at noon by field workers.

The corn sticks and corn muffins featured on Williamsburg tavern menus are refinements of pone, being made from a medium batter and baked in molds in a hot oven.

INDIAN CORN MUFFINS

(*1 dozen*)

1 cup corn meal
1 cup sifted all-purpose flour
1 teaspoon salt
2½ teaspoons baking powder

1 cup milk
2 eggs, beaten
2 tablespoons shortening,
   melted

Preheat oven to 400° F.
Sift dry ingredients into mixing bowl.
Combine milk with eggs and add to the dry ingredients.
Add shortening and stir until blended.
Pour into 2-inch muffin tins and bake at 400° F. for 20 minutes.

INDIAN CORN STICKS

(*1 dozen*)

Follow recipe for Indian Corn Muffins (*above*).
Bake batter in bread-stick pans.

CHRISTIANA CAMPBELL'S TAVERN
SPOON BREAD

(*8 servings*)

Spoon bread, or batter bread, is a custardy corn bread served soufflé-hot from the dish, preferably earthenware, in which it is baked. It is said that the recipe "just happened" when a mixture used to make a corn bread enriched by milk and eggs was left forgotten in a hot oven. That probably was a day in the nineteenth century, and Virginians have ever since made spoon bread one of their favored foods. It is excellent served with herring roe, bacon, or fried apples.

1½ cups water   1½ teaspoons sugar
2 cups milk   2 tablespoons butter
1½ cups corn meal   5 eggs
1⅓ teaspoons salt   1 tablespoon baking powder

Preheat oven to 350°F.

Grease a large, shallow baking dish.

Combine water and milk and heat to simmer.

Add corn meal, salt, sugar, and butter, and stir over medium heat until the mixture is thickened, about 5 minutes. Remove from heat.

Beat eggs with baking powder until very light and fluffy, then add to corn meal mixture. Mix well.

Pour into prepared dish and bake at 350°F. for 45 to 50 minutes.

Serve hot.

GRITS SOUFFLE

(6 servings)

2 cups milk   2 tablespoons butter, melted
½ cup instant grits   ½ teaspoon sugar
1 teaspoon salt   3 eggs, separated
½ teaspoon baking powder

Preheat oven to 375° F.

Grease 1½-quart casserole or 1½-quart soufflé dish.

Scald milk, add grits, and cook until thick, stirring constantly.

Add salt, baking powder, butter, and sugar; mix well.

Beat egg yolks and add to grits.

Whip egg whites until they hold soft peaks; fold in.

Pour into prepared dish.

Bake at 375° F. for 30 minutes.

Serve hot.

Note: Just before folding in the egg whites, ½ cup grated sharp cheese, and a dash of Tabasco sauce can be added to make an excellent variation of the above recipe.

CHRISTIANA CAMPBELL'S TAVERN PUMPKIN FRITTERS

(1½ dozen)

1 egg
½ cup sugar
½ teaspoon salt
1½ cups canned pumpkin
1 cup all-purpose flour
1 teaspoon baking powder
¼ teaspoon baking soda

2 teaspoons pumpkin pie spice
½ teaspoon ginger
1 tablespoon margarine,
  melted
1 teaspoon vanilla
confectioner's sugar

Beat eggs, sugar, and salt until very light and fluffy.
Blend in pumpkin.
Sift flour, baking powder, and baking soda together. Beat into egg mixture.
Add spices, margarine, and vanilla. Mix well.
Drop by tablespoonsful onto well-greased hot griddle or fry in deep hot fat a teaspoonful at a time.
Watch carefully—these scorch easily.
Sprinkle with confectioner's sugar.
Pumpkin fritters taste best served with fresh fish.

SALLY LUNN

Sally Lunn, a pride of southern cooks, is named after a young lady who in the eighteenth century sold the warm crumbly bread that bears her name by "crying" it in the streets of England's fashionable spa, Bath. A "respectable baker and musician" bought her business and wrote a song about her. The song is forgotten but Sally has a place in the *Oxford English Dictionary*, and hers was a household name in the colonies.

1 cup milk
½ cup shortening
4 cups sifted all-purpose flour,
  divided

⅓ cup sugar
2 teaspoons salt
2 packages active dry yeast
3 eggs

Preheat oven to 350° F. 10 minutes before Sally Lunn is ready to be baked.

Grease a 10-inch tube cake pan or a bundt pan.

Heat the milk, shortening, and ¼ cup water until very warm—about 120° F. Shortening does not need to melt.

Blend 1⅓ cups flour, the sugar, salt, and dry yeast in a large mixing bowl.

Blend warm liquids into flour mixture. Beat with an electric mixer at medium speed about 2 minutes, scraping the sides of the bowl occasionally.

Gradually add ⅔ cup of the remaining flour and the eggs and beat at high speed for 2 minutes.

Add the remaining flour and mix well. Batter will be thick, but not stiff.

Cover and let rise in a warm, draft-free place (about 85° F.) until double in bulk—about 1 hour and 15 minutes.

Beat dough down with a spatula or at lowest speed on an electric mixer and turn into prepared pan.

Cover and let rise in a warm, draft-free place until increased in bulk one-third to one-half—about 30 minutes.

Bake 40 to 50 minutes at 350° F.

Run knife around the center and outer edges of the bread and turn onto a plate to cool.

MRS. BOOTH'S BISCUIT MIX
(*4½ cups*)

3 cups self-rising flour	*1 cup shortening*
1½ teaspoons baking powder	*milk*
1 tablespoon sugar	*melted butter*

Preheat oven to 450° F. 10 minutes before biscuits are to go in.

Grease a cookie sheet.

Sift the dry ingredients into a mixing bowl.

Cut in shortening with knives or pastry blender until evenly distributed.

Store in covered container in refrigerator.

For 6 biscuits, 2 inches in diameter, combine 1 cup mix with enough milk to moisten.

Knead lightly on floured surface 5 or 6 times.

Roll out ½ inch thick for high biscuits; ¼ inch thick for thin, crusty biscuits. Cut with a biscuit cutter.

Place on prepared cookie sheet and brush tops with melted butter or milk. Space dough close together for soft biscuits; 1 inch apart for crusty ones.

Bake at 450° F. for 8 to 10 minutes or until golden brown.

PECAN WAFFLES

(6–8 servings)

In twelfth-century England holy bread was small, especially stamped wafers made from a fine-textured flour. Ordinary wafers, or waffles, were larger, thicker, and more substantial. Chaucer mentions them in the *Canterbury Tales*, and many a poet who bought his wafer piping hot on the street or at a stall beside the church door sang its praises. Homemade wafers had a sweetened sauce poured over them. They were baked in irons, either round or square, which were long-handled for holding over the coals of an open fire.

For more than 250 years after King Henry VIII's break with Rome, wafers were forgotten in Great Britain—until some Dutch migrants to Paisley, Scotland, introduced their *wafelijzer*, which an English cookbook called "The Right Dutch Wafer," and which we in America now call the waffle.

Thomas Jefferson first tasted waffles in Holland in 1789 and there bought a pair of waffle irons with tongs for one and one-third Dutch florins.

2⅔ cups sifted all-purpose flour
3 tablespoons sugar
4 teaspoons baking powder
1 teaspoon salt
4 eggs, separated

2⅔ cups milk
½ cup plus 1 tablespoon butter, melted
⅓ cup chopped pecans

Sift the dry ingredients together.

Beat egg yolks until thick.

Combine beaten yolks with milk and melted butter, and stir into dry ingredients.

Add pecans, mixing only until blended.
Beat egg whites until stiff and fold into batter.
Bake in hot waffle iron.

(4–5 servings)

1½ cups sifted all-purpose flour	*3 eggs, separated*
1½ tablespoons sugar	*1½ cups milk*
2½ teaspoons baking powder	*5 tablespoons butter, melted*
½ teaspoon salt	*¼ cup chopped pecans*

Follow instructions above.

MANCHET BREAD

Wheat flour has always been acknowledged as the best for making white bread. England's bakers, from the fourteenth century onwards, called bread made from fine quality wheat flour manchet bread.

Today many people, especially young people, are showing increased interest in foods that contain no preservatives. Chiefly for this reason, Colonial Williamsburg has added a quality bread made from a fine unbleached wheat flour, stone-ground as it used to be in colonial times, to its menus, and revived the name manchet for it.

3½ to 4 cups sifted unbleached natural flour, divided	*1½ teaspoons salt*
	1 cup warm water
1 package (¼ ounce) active dry yeast	*¼ cup butter*
	1 egg, room temperature
2 tablespoons sugar	

Combine 1 cup flour with dry yeast, sugar, and salt in large bowl of mixer; mix thoroughly.

Heat water with butter over low heat until very warm (120° to 130° F.).

Gradually add liquids to dry ingredients. Beat for 2 minutes at medium speed, scraping bowl occasionally.

Add ½ cup flour, or enough flour to make thick batter. Add egg and beat on high speed for 2 minutes. Keep scraping the bowl.

113

Stir in enough additional flour to make a soft dough, approximately 1½ cups.

Turn dough onto lightly-floured board; knead until smooth and elastic, about 8 to 10 minutes, using remaining flour as needed. *Kneading time is important.*

Place in greased bowl, turning to grease top. Cover with moist cloth and let rise in warm, draft-free place (about 85° F.) until double in bulk—about 1 to 1½ hours. Keep cover cloth moist.

Grease a 9¼ x 5¼ x 2¾-inch loaf pan.

Punch dough down; turn out onto lightly-floured board. Cover; let rest 15 minutes. Roll into uniform thickness in a 9 x 12-inch rectangle. Beginning with upper 9-inch side, roll towards you, jelly-roll style. Seal with thumbs or heel of hand. Seal ends; fold sealed ends under. Be careful not to tear dough. Place in prepared pan.

Cover with moist cloth, let rise in warm, draft-free place until double in bulk, about 1 hour.

When dough is near end of rising time, preheat oven to 350° F.

Place loaf in oven on center shelf and bake at 350° F. for 40 minutes, or until done.

Remove from pan immediately and cool on rack.

WILLIAMSBURG INN
YORKSHIRE PUDDING

(6–8 servings)

There are probably as many ways to make Yorkshire Pudding as there are to make bread. The word "pudding" implies a somewhat solid dish, but Yorkshire Pudding should be light, puffy, crisp, and brown. It should be ready to serve at the same moment as the beef, for which it is the superb accompaniment. Colonial Williamsburg adds a refinement of former days that most housewives cannot manage today—the meat drips onto the pudding as it finishes cooking.

2 *eggs*
1 *cup milk*
1 *cup all-purpose flour*
salt and pepper to taste

pinch nutmeg
½ *cup melted fat* or *beef drippings, divided*

Preheat oven to 425° F. 10 minutes before pudding is ready to go in.

Beat eggs for 1 minute with an electric mixer on highest speed.

Add milk and gradually beat in the flour.

Add seasoning and 2 tablespoons of melted fat or drippings and beat 1 minute on highest speed. Let stand at room temperature at least 30 minutes.

Place remaining fat in a 7½-inch black skillet to cover the bottom by ⅛ inch and heat in the oven until sizzling hot.

Add mixture and bake at 425° F. for 30 minutes.

Reduce heat to 350° F. and bake an additional 10 to 15 minutes.

Do not be dismayed when center falls—this is characteristic of Yorkshire Pudding.

Note: It would be helpful to save drippings from previous roasts to use in making this dish.

WILLIAMSBURG INN POPOVERS

(*8–10 servings*)

Liberally grease 8 or 10 custard cups.

Follow recipe for Yorkshire Pudding *(page 114)* but omit the pepper. Butter can be substituted for drippings.

Pour batter into prepared, heated custard cups, filling not more than ⅓ full.

Bake at 425° F. for 30 minutes, then turn off oven. Allow popovers to remain in oven 5 to 10 minutes longer.

Serve immediately.

115

Desserts

Wrote an eighteenth-century poet:

> 'Tis the Desert that graces all the Feast,
> For an ill end disparages the rest. . . . .

The dessert was the pride and joy of colonial Virginia's housewives. A "Collation of Sweetmeats" was customarily served at plantation house balls or on great occasions at the Governor's Palace, or sometimes in the Capitol. William Byrd II set down in his diary:

> About 7 o'clock the company went in coaches from the Governor's house to the capitol where the Governor opened the ball with a French dance with my wife. . . . Then we danced country dances for an hour and the company was carried into another room where was a very fine collation of sweetmeats.

On one occasion the long tables bore one hundred dishes of creams and jellies, confectionery of all sorts, candied fruits, and sugared nuts.

In the *Virginia Gazette* of October 6, 1738, Mrs. Stagg of Williamsburg gave notice that she had for sale hartshorn and calves-feet jellies, fresh every Tuesday and Friday:

> Also Curran Jellies, & many other sorts of Fruit Jellies: Mackaroons, and Savoy Biscakes; and all sorts of Confectionary, in small Quantities, or large if wanted, every Day, at very reasonable Rates. She has a considerable Quantity of choice Barbadoes Sweet-meats, which are to be sold in small Pots, or a smaller Quantity.

Those were the days of the flummery and the floating island, the first being made of milk, flour, and eggs and the other of little cakes topped with egg white and set afloat on a sea of syllabub. The syllabub

116

itself was a standard drink or dish, rich or simple, fundamentally of milk or cream with wine, sugar, and other flavorings, sometimes curdled and sometimes "whipt." The simplest variety was Syllabub-under-the-Cow, made in a quick trip to the cow barn to draw a fine warm froth of milk directly into a bowl of wine. Its name was derived from "Sill," the name of its French wine, and from "bub," the Elizabethan nickname for a bubbling drink.

Gone now are the flummeries, the floating islands, the syllabubs. No longer are there enough hands, nor is there enough time, for the making of elaborate creams and cakes except by professionals. Too, tastes have changed. We have become content to sample one dessert at a time—ice cream or sherbet, pudding, cream or mousse, or pie—and to watch our weight.

CHRISTIANA CAMPBELL'S TAVERN
TIPSY SQUIRE
(*10 servings*)

This is the American version of the nineteenth-century English tipsy cake. Although Tipsy Squire is fully capable of justifying its name, gourmets will not overlook the squire's noble counterpart, the English Trifle.

The Trifle is no trifling matter. Many versions exist, yet for the true trifle—one of the most exotic of desserts—there is no simplified substitute.

Colonial Williamsburg uses fresh fruit rather than jam in its ingredients, but in every other particular uses the prescribed ingredients for the classic dish. The purists' rules are also followed: that only sherry—no other wine—be used for flavoring, and that the trifle be made in a crystal dish.

½ cup shortening
1 cup sugar
2 eggs
2¼ cups sifted all-purpose flour
3 teaspoons baking powder
½ teaspoon salt

¾ cup milk
1 teaspoon vanilla
SHERRY CUSTARD (*below*)
whipped cream
toasted slivered almonds

Preheat oven to 350° F.

Grease and lightly flour a 9 x 9 x 2-inch or 7½ x 11½ x 2-inch baking pan.

Cream shortening and sugar.

Add eggs and beat until lemon-colored and fluffy.

Add sifted dry ingredients alternately with milk, beating well after each addition.

Add vanilla with last addition of milk.

Pour into prepared cake pan.

Bake at 350° F. for 35 to 40 minutes or until cake tests done.

Cool on cake rack before cutting into portions.

To serve, place portion of cake in a dessert bowl and pour Sherry Custard over it.

Garnish with sweetened whipped cream and toasted almonds.

SHERRY CUSTARD

1 quart milk
¾ cup sugar
3 tablespoons cornstarch
⅛ teaspoon salt

3 egg yolks
1 egg
1 teaspoon rum flavoring
½ cup cream sherry

Cook milk, sugar, cornstarch, and salt over medium heat, stirring constantly, until slightly thickened.

Beat egg yolks and 1 whole egg.

Add 1 cup hot milk mixture to beaten egg yolks, stir and return to hot milk.

Continue cooking, stirring constantly, but do not boil, until of custard consistency.

Add rum flavoring and sherry.

Cool and serve over cake.

Note: Sometimes, in spite of every precaution, custard separates. When this happens, remove custard from heat immediately and place in a bowl of cracked ice. Beat rapidly until smoothness is restored. Custard will be slightly thinner.

ENGLISH FRUIT TRIFLE
(8–10 servings)

2 cups Custard Sauce (page 122), divided
1 teaspoon unflavored gelatin
2 dozen ladyfingers or 1 layer of sponge cake cut into fingers, divided
1 cup strawberry jelly or jam, divided
rind of 1 lemon, grated and divided

1 cup dry sherry, divided
3 tablespoons brandy, divided
fresh fruits in season, divided
1 dozen macaroons crushed and divided
2 cups whipping cream
½ cup slivered almonds, toasted

Prepare Custard Sauce. Add 1 teaspoon unflavored gelatin, softened, to custard while cooking, if desired.

Coat ½ of the ladyfingers with ½ cup strawberry jelly or jam, place in the bottom of a crystal bowl 8 inches in diameter and 3½-inches deep, and sprinkle with ½ lemon rind.

Sprinkle liberally with ½ cup sherry and ½ of the brandy.

Cover with a layer of ½ of the fresh fruit and ½ of the macaroons. Allow to stand an hour or so.

Pour ½ of the Custard Sauce over top, repeat layers of ladyfingers, jelly or jam, lemon rind, sherry, brandy, fresh fruit and remaining macaroons. Repeat custard layer. Chill.

Just before serving, top with whipped cream and slivered almonds.

AMBROSIA
(6 servings)

3 fresh oranges
3 fresh grapefruit
½ small fresh pineapple
⅓ cup orange juice

¼ cup light corn syrup
½ cup flaked or fresh coconut, shredded

119

Peel and section oranges and grapefruit.

Peel and dice pineapple and mix it with the orange and grapefruit sections.

Combine orange juice and syrup.

Divide fruit mixture into 6 sherbet glasses, pour juice over fruit, and top with coconut.

Note: Whole blueberries or sliced strawberries can be added to above for color as well as flavor.

Also note: A little dry sherry can be mixed with the orange juice for a different flavor. If sherry is added, allow the mixture to ripen overnight.

FRESH STRAWBERRY MOUSSE

(*8–10 servings*)

This is certainly a dish to set before a queen, as indeed it was at the dinner given in honor of Queen Elizabeth II and Prince Philip at the Williamsburg Inn. And there was something especially appropriate in the choice of this dessert.

When the first Virginia settlers stepped ashore in the spring of 1607, they found strawberries in a little plot of ground in a clearing of the forest. They were reminded instantly of home, only they were "foure times bigger and better" than those in England. One enthusiast claimed that they were so thick on the ground that men's shoes were stained red with their juice as they walked among them.

1 pint strawberries
2 packages (3 ounces each)
   strawberry flavor gelatin

¼ cup sugar
1 pint whipping cream

Crush the strawberries and drain the juice, reserve. Add enough water to the juice to make 1½ cups.

Bring the juice to a boil and stir in gelatin; dissolve and cool. Add strawberries and sugar.

Whip cream until it stands in soft peaks and fold into strawberry mixture.

Pour mixture into a 2-quart ring mold or 1½-quart soufflé dish with a 2-inch collar.

120

Chill several hours or overnight.

Note: Two packages (10 ounces each) of frozen strawberries can be substituted for the fresh strawberries. Omit sugar if frozen berries are used.

KING'S ARMS TAVERN OLD-FASHIONED RAISIN RICE PUDDING

(8 servings)

4 eggs	1 ½ teaspoons vanilla
¾ cup sugar	1 tablespoon butter, melted
2 cups milk	1 teaspoon nutmeg
1 ⅓ cups cooked rice	⅔ cup seedless raisins
1 ½ teaspoons lemon juice	

Preheat oven to 350° F.

Grease 2 quart casserole.

Combine eggs, sugar, and milk and beat well.

Fold in rice, lemon juice, vanilla, melted butter, nutmeg, and raisins.

Pour into prepared casserole and put the dish in a pan of boiling water.

Bake at 350° F. for approximately 45 minutes or until custard is set.

WINE JELLY MOLD WITH CUSTARD SAUCE

(10–12 servings)

4 envelopes unflavored gelatin	2½ cups burgundy
2 cups sugar	CUSTARD SAUCE *(page 122)* or
6 tablespoons lemon juice	whipped cream and red
rind of 3 lemons, grated	glazed cherries

Soften gelatin in 1½ cups cold water for 5 minutes.

Dissolve sugar in 1 quart of hot water and bring to a boil, then remove from heat.

Add lemon juice, rind, and softened gelatin, allow to set 5 minutes, and then strain mixture through cheesecloth.

Add burgundy, stirring gently to avoid making air bubbles.

Pour slowly into 8-cup mold and chill several hours or until firm.

Unmold onto chilled serving dish.

Serve with Custard Sauce or garnish lightly with whipped cream and red glazed cherries.

CUSTARD SAUCE

1½ tablespoons cornstarch *½ cup sugar*
2 cups light cream, divided *1 teaspoon vanilla*
4 egg yolks

Dissolve cornstarch in ¼ cup cream.

Beat egg yolks until light, then combine with cornstarch.

Heat remaining cream, taking care not to boil, and add sugar.

Pour 1 cup hot cream and sugar over egg mixture, stirring constantly.

Return cream to low heat, stir in egg-cream mixture, and continue to stir and cook 5 minutes until sauce is slightly thickened.

Add vanilla, blend thoroughly, and cool.

WILLIAMSBURG LODGE
BAVARIAN CREAM

(4–5 servings)

1 envelope unflavored gelatin *1 cup milk*
4 egg yolks *1 cup whipping cream*
dash of salt *2 teaspoons vanilla*
½ cup sugar

Soften gelatin in ¼ cup cold water; set aside.

Mix egg yolks, salt, and sugar together in the top of a double boiler.

Gradually blend in milk and cook over hot water, stirring constantly, until thick and smooth.

Add softened gelatin, stirring until dissolved; cool.

Whip cream, add vanilla, and fold in gently.

Spoon into 1-quart mold or 4 or 5 sherbet or parfait glasses. Chill.

Note: For a lighter Bavarian Cream, beat the egg whites and add before the whipped cream. This will make 8 servings.

CHOCOLATE BAVARIAN CREAM

Follow instructions for Williamsburg Lodge Bavarian Cream (page 122).

Decrease vanilla to 1 teaspoon.

Before cooling the egg-gelatin mixture, add 2 ounces unsweetened chocolate, melted.

LIQUEUR BAVARIAN CREAM

Follow instructions for Williamsburg Lodge Bavarian Cream (page 122).

Omit vanilla.

Add 2 tablespoons of any flavor liqueur to the whipped cream.

APRICOT BAVARIAN CREAM

(*8 servings*)

1 package orange flavor
  gelatin
¼ cup sugar
1 cup apricot juice
1 cup crushed apricots,
  drained

¼ teaspoon almond extract
1 cup whipping cream
2 tablespoons brandy

Dissolve gelatin in 1 cup hot water. Add sugar and apricot juice.

Chill until cold and syrupy. Add apricots and almond extract.

Whip cream until it stands in soft peaks. Fold into gelatin mixture.

Chill until almost firm, then stir in brandy.

Spoon into sherbet or parfait glasses and chill until firm.

STRAWBERRY BAVARIAN CREAM

Follow instructions for Apricot Bavarian Cream (page 123).

Substitute strawberry-flavored gelatin, strawberry juice, and drained crushed strawberries. Omit brandy.

WILLIAMSBURG LODGE
MOCHA VELVET CREAM

(6–8 servings)

1 envelope unflavored gelatin	*2½ tablespoons instant coffee*
1½ cups milk, divided	*4 eggs, separated*
¾ cup sugar, divided	*1 teaspoon vanilla*
½ teaspoon salt	*1 cup whipping cream*

Sprinkle gelatin over ¼ cup milk; set aside to soften.

Blend ½ cup sugar, salt, coffee, and egg yolks in the top of a double boiler.

Gradually add remaining milk. Cook over hot water, stirring constantly, until thickened and smooth.

Add softened gelatin, cook, stirring constantly, until dissolved.

Remove from heat, add vanilla, and chill until slightly thickened.

Reserve 1 tablespoon of the remaining sugar for the whipping cream, and beat the egg whites with the rest of the sugar until they are stiff but not dry. Fold into gelatin mixture.

Whip cream and gently fold half of it into the gelatin-egg white mixture.

Spoon into 6 to 8 individual dessert dishes and chill until set.

Top with remaining whipped cream sweetened with reserved sugar.

124

Ice Creams and Sherbets

Sherbets were the forerunners of ice cream. The Chinese taught the Hindus, the Persians, and the Arabs the art of making water ices, or sherbets. A Sicilian who got around introduced them into France about 1660 and later opened in Paris a café specializing in sherbets. Sherbets became the rage, and in due course ice creams followed. Soon there were around 250 shops and restaurants in Paris that were officially licensed to make and sell ice creams and water ices.

Wealthy Marylanders appear to have learned about ice cream before Virginians did. Governor Thomas Bladen's French wife may have introduced them there. On May 19, 1744, William Black, a Virginian on official business in Annapolis, attended a dinner at the governor's mansion and later reported:

> We were Received by his Excellency and his Lady in the Hall, where we were an hour Entertain'd by the Governor, with some Glasses of Punch in the intervals of the Discourse; then the Scene was chang'd to a Dining Room, where you saw a Table in the most Splendent manner set out with a Great Variety of Dishes, all serv'd up in the most Elegant way, after which came a Dessert no less Curious; Among the Rarities of which it was Compos'd, was some fine Ice Cream which, with the Strawberries and Milk, eat most Deliciously.

Governor Francis Fauquier of Virginia wrote his brother that in July, 1758, a hailstorm provided a supply of ice which he used to cool wine and to freeze cream.

In May 1784, George Washington recorded in his diary that he had spent one pound, thirteen shillings, and four pence on a "cream machine for ice."

In a letter dated August 16, 1799, Mrs. Anne Blair Banister wrote from Shannon Hill to her niece: "Yesterday we were at Mr. Baylors, & made myself sick with Ice-Creams, Water Melons, Plumbs &c—(so has Mr. Cary. . . . Alas! so much frigidity does not suit us old folks)."

VANILLA ICE CREAM

(1 gallon)

2 tablespoons cornstarch
2 quarts milk, divided
4 eggs, separated
2 cups sugar

½ teaspoon salt
2 teaspoons vanilla
1 pint whipping cream

Dissolve cornstarch in 1 cup milk.

Heat remaining milk and add cornstarch, stirring constantly.

Add well-beaten egg yolks and sugar.

Stir constantly and cook over low heat until mixture coats metal spoon.

Cool several hours or overnight in the refrigerator, if possible.

When ready to freeze, beat egg whites, salt and vanilla to a froth and add to the chilled milk mixture.

Stir in cream and pour mixture into a 5-quart freezer container, following the manufacturer's directions for freezing.

CHRISTIANA CAMPBELL'S TAVERN
FIG ICE CREAM

(3 quarts)

4 eggs, separated
1¼ cups sugar, divided
2 cups milk, scalded
3 tablespoons lemon juice

1 pint light cream
½ cup cream sherry
1 teaspoon vanilla
1 quart figs, crushed or *puréed*

Beat egg yolks and ½ cup plus 2 tablespoons sugar.

Add milk slowly, stirring constantly.

Cook over low heat until quite hot, but do not boil.

Combine egg whites with remaining sugar and beat to a light froth.

Pour cooked egg-milk mixture into egg whites, stirring constantly.

Stir in lemon juice.

Add cream, sherry, vanilla, and figs, blending well.

Pour mixture into a 5-quart freezer container, following the manufacturer's directions for freezing.

KING'S ARMS TAVERN
GREENGAGE PLUM ICE CREAM

(*3 quarts*)

Greengage Plum Ice Cream was a happy accident. One of Williamsburg's taverns happened to be out of the usual flavorings for ice cream that day. The greengage plum came to the rescue, and now flavors one of the most popular ice creams at the King's Arms, where it has become a specialty.

"All plums," said the herbalist Nicholas Culpeper, "are under Venus, and are like women—some better and some worse." The greengage plum is the accepted queen of plums; a wilding of the Caucasus, it wandered through Italy and France to become known there as Reine Claude, after the wife of François I. Reine Claude kept wandering and in America left an offspring known as the Jefferson greengage.

5 eggs, separated
1½ cups sugar, divided
2 cups milk
3 cups fresh or *canned (1 pound, 12 ounces) greengage plums, drained and stoned*

1½ pints light cream
⅓ cup lemon juice
green food coloring

Beat egg yolks together with 1 cup sugar.

Heat milk almost to boiling, and pour 1 cup over beaten egg yolks, stirring until well blended.

Return egg-milk mixture to hot milk and cook, but do not boil, over medium heat, stirring constantly, until mixture coats metal spoon; cool.

Beat egg whites with ½ cup sugar and, when egg mixture is cool, combine the two, mixing well.

Purée plums in a blender at low speed 3 to 5 seconds or rub through a sieve.

127

Add the plums, cream, and lemon juice gradually to the egg mixture.

Add green food coloring, a few drops at a time, until desired pistachio green tint is achieved.

Pour mixture into a 5-quart freezer container, following the manufacturer's directions for freezing.

Note: Ice cream should be allowed to "ripen" at least four hours after freezing to bring out the delicate greengage plum flavor.

Also note: If fresh greengage plums are used, they should be blanched 60 seconds in hot water before skins are removed.

CHOWNING'S TAVERN
BLACK WALNUT ICE CREAM

(1½ quarts)

Farmers of the eastern seaboard states, where the black walnut is native, spent many a winter evening before the open fire cracking and eating walnuts. A nut of such fine taste just had to find its way into ice cream.

8 egg yolks	*2 cups whipping cream*
1¼ cups sugar	*1 teaspoon black walnut*
dash of salt	*flavoring*
2 cups milk	*1 cup black walnuts, chopped*

Beat egg yolks with sugar until creamy; add salt.

Bring milk and cream almost to boiling; remove from heat and pour slowly into egg mixture, stirring constantly.

Return to low heat, stirring constantly to avoid scorching, but do not boil. Add black walnut flavoring. Heat to scalding.

Pour mixture into a 1-gallon freezer container, following the manufacturer's directions for freezing.

When dasher is removed, add black walnuts, stirring to distribute evenly.

Pack as freezing instructions direct and allow to "ripen" at least 3 hours before serving.

ORANGE SHERBET

(2 quarts)

1½ cups sugar
1 cup light corn syrup
1 can (12 ounces) frozen
   orange juice concentrate

1 can (6 ounces) frozen
   lemonade concentrate
rind of 1 orange, grated

Boil sugar in 6 cups of water for 5 minutes.

Add corn syrup, juices, and rind.

Cool and strain. Pour mixture into a 1-gallon freezer container, following the manufacturer's directions for freezing.

RASPBERRY ICE

(3 quarts)

4 packages (10 ounces each)
   frozen red raspberries
1 can (6 ounces) frozen
   lemonade concentrate

2¼ cups sugar, divided
1 envelope unflavored gelatin
2 egg whites

Thaw raspberries, purée in blender 4 to 5 seconds, press through a sieve to remove seeds, and combine with thawed lemonade concentrate.

Mix 4 cups water and 2 cups sugar and boil over medium heat for 5 minutes. Cool.

Soften gelatin in ¼ cup water. Stir softened gelatin into cooling sugar syrup; continue stirring until gelatin is dissolved.

Combine sugar and raspberry mixtures.

Beat egg whites with remaining sugar and add to raspberry mixture. Blend well.

Pour mixture into a 1-gallon freezer container, following the manufacturer's directions for freezing.

⋙⋘

Pastries

S ome liked bread made of wheat flour and others preferred it of corn meal, but there was one reason why early Virginia housewives had to have wheat flour on hand. Corn meal is no good for pastry-making; the dough does not "spread." After all, early Virginians were almost all of English stock, and what Englishman would be without his pie—a dish of meat, fowl, fish, fruit, or vegetables enclosed or covered with a layer of paste and baked.

Properly a pie, like the English garden, is enclosed. A tart is open and smaller, brought into England no doubt from the Continent. The American pie, as we know it, is a compromise between the pie and the tart: it is not baked as it so often was in England—or in Mrs. Campbell's tavern—in a deep pie dish, but when it contains the Old World fruits of apple, cherry, peach, or apricot, it is enclosed with crust in a pie pan. Pies made of New World pumpkin and pecan are open like tarts.

PASTRY CRUST MIX

(4½ cups)

3 cups all-purpose flour   1 cup shortening
1 teaspoon salt   ice water
2 teaspoons sugar

Mix dry ingredients together.

Blend in shortening with knives or pastry blender until mixture is of pebbly consistency.

Store in covered container in refrigerator.

When needed, measure out these amounts:

	Single Crust	Double Crust
8-inch pie	1 to 1¼ cups	2 to 2¼ cups
9-inch pie	1½ cups	2½ cups
10-inch pie	1¾ cups	2¾ cups
12 tart shells	2¾ cups	

Moisten pastry mix with enough ice water to hold dough together when pushed lightly with a fork.

Roll out on lightly floured board or pastry cloth.

Note: When recipe calls for prebaked shell or shells, line pan with dough, prick well with a fork, and bake at 425° F. for 12 to 15 minutes or until golden brown.

(9 cups)

7 cups all-purpose flour   1 pound shortening
1 tablespoon salt   ice water
5 teaspoons sugar

Follow instructions above.

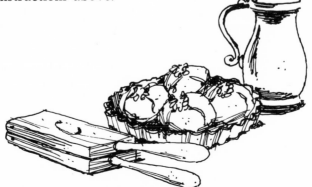

131

APPLE PIE

(one 9-inch pie)

Apple pie is the beginning of the kitchen alphabet for English-speaking children the world over, and for many a man, as for many a boy, it is the pie of pies. A distinct line is drawn by good cooks between a cooking and an eating apple, or, as purists say, between a culinary and a dessert apple. Old varieties are hard to come by. Rome Beauty is Colonial Williamsburg's favorite culinary apple.

PASTRY CRUST MIX *for 9-inch double crust pie (page 131)*
1¼ to 1½ cups sugar
⅛ teaspcon salt
¾ teaspoon cinnamon
½ teaspoon nutmeg

2 tablespoons all-purpose flour
6 to 8 tart apples (2 to 2½ pounds), peeled and sliced
lemon juice (optional)
½ teaspoon lemon rind, grated
1 to 2 tablespoons butter

Preheat oven to 425° F.
Roll pastry for bottom crust over rolling pin for ease in lining pan. Cover pastry for the top crust while filling the pie to keep it moist.
Mix dry ingredients together in large bowl.
Add sliced apples and mix to coat.
Place apple slices in pan, laying slices first along the outside and then working toward the center until bottom of pastry is covered.
Continue placing in same way until pan is filled.
Sprinkle with lemon juice and rind and dot with butter.
Moisten edge of bottom crust.
Roll top crust around rolling pin, unroll over apple filling, and trim to ½-inch larger than pie pan. Press edges firmly together, flute, and slash vents in the center of the crust.
Bake at 425° F. for 50 to 60 minutes until apples are done and crust is golden brown.

APPLE DUMPLINGS

(6 dumplings)

PASTRY CRUST MIX *for 10-inch double crust pie (page 131)*
6 *whole, large apples, peeled and cored*

1½ *cups sugar, divided*
¾ *teaspoon cinnamon, divided*
¼ *teaspoon nutmeg*
6 *tablespoons butter, divided*

Preheat oven to 450° F. 10 minutes before dumplings are ready to be baked.

Roll out pastry ⅛-inch thick and cut into six 7-inch squares.

Place an apple in center of each square.

Fill apples with a mixture of ½ cup sugar, ½ teaspoon cinnamon, ¼ teaspoon nutmeg, and 2 tablespoons butter.

Moisten edges of pastry with cold water and fold up around apples, pressing edges together to seal firmly. Prick pastry in several places.

Chill 1 hour.

Combine remaining sugar, cinnamon, butter, and 2 cups hot water and boil 5 minutes.

Place apples in 9 x 12-inch baking dish and bake at 450° F. 10 minutes.

Reduce heat to 350° F., pour syrup over apples and bake 35 minutes, basting occasionally.

CHRISTIANA CAMPBELL'S TAVERN RUM CREAM PIE

(one 9-inch pie)

1 *envelope unflavored gelatin*
5 *egg yolks*
1 *cup sugar*
⅓ *cup dark rum*

1½ *cups whipping cream*
CRUMB CRUST *(page 134)*
unsweetened chocolate

Soften gelatin in ½ cup cold water. Place over low heat and bring almost to a boil, stirring to dissolve.

Beat egg yolks and sugar until very light.

Stir gelatin into egg mixture; cool.

Gradually add rum, beating constantly.

Whip cream until it stands in soft peaks and fold into gelatin mixture.

Cool until mixture begins to set, then spoon into Crumb Crust and chill until firm enough to cut.

Grate unsweetened chocolate over top before serving.

CRUMB CRUST

2¼ cups graham cracker   2 tablespoons sugar
  crumbs   ½ teaspoon cinnamon
½ cup butter, melted

Combine ingredients and press into 9-inch pie pan; chill.

EGGNOG PIE

(one 9-inch pie)

PASTRY CRUST MIX *for 9-inch*   ¾ cup sugar, divided
  pie (page 131) or CRUMB   3 eggs, separated
  CRUST *(above)*   ¼ cup light or dark rum
1 envelope unflavored gelatin   1 cup whipping cream
1 cup milk   nutmeg

Prepare and bake pie shell, or chill Crumb Crust.

Soften gelatin in ¼ cup water; set aside.

Bring milk and ½ cup sugar to a boil.

Beat egg yolks.

Add ½ cup hot milk and sugar mixture to eggs, stir, and return egg mixture to the remaining hot milk and sugar mixture.

Cook, stirring, but not boiling, until custard coats metal spoon.

Stir in gelatin and rum.

134

Cool in refrigerator until mixture begins to set.

Beat egg whites with 3 tablespoons sugar until soft peaks form. Fold into the custard.

Whip cream and fold in 1 cup.

Spoon into pie shell.

Beat 1 tablespoon sugar into remaining whipped cream, and spread on pie.

Sprinkle with nutmeg and chill until ready to serve.

Note: This pie freezes well. It needs to be removed from freezer only a few minutes before serving.

LEMON MERINGUE PIE

(one 9-inch pie)

PASTRY CRUST MIX *for 9-inch pie (page 131)*
1¾ cups sugar, divided
½ cup cornstarch
½ teaspoon salt, divided

3 eggs, separated
⅓ cup lemon juice
5 teaspoons lemon rind, grated
2 tablespoons butter

Prepare and bake pie shell.

Preheat oven to 350° F. 10 minutes before pie is ready to go in.

Measure and reserve 6 tablespoons sugar for meringue.

Mix together in a saucepan the remaining sugar, cornstarch, 1½ cups water, and ¼ teaspoon salt.

When sugar is dissolved and cornstarch is completely blended, cook over medium heat, stirring constantly, until mixture is smooth and almost transparent, about 3 minutes.

Beat egg yolks and lemon juice together and add about ½ cup hot mixture. Stir to mix well.

Add to hot cornstarch mixture, stirring constantly until thick, 3 to 4 minutes.

Add rind and butter, remove from heat, and stir well.

Place plastic wrap directly on surface of lemon filling to prevent film from forming while it cools.

When cold, spoon into cooled pie shell.

Make meringue by beating egg whites and ¼ teaspoon salt until soft peaks form. Gradually add 6 tablespoons sugar to egg whites and continue beating at high speed until firm, glossy peaks are formed.

Pile meringue on top of filling, taking care to spread meringue to edges of crust to seal and prevent shrinking.

Bake at 350° F. for 12 to 15 minutes or until meringue is delicately browned.

Allow pie to cool on rack for at least 2 hours before cutting.

Note: For a less tart pie, substitute ½ cup lemon juice and 1 teaspoon lemon rind for the quantities called for above.

LEMON CHESS TARTS

(12 small tarts)

This originally was a cake or a tart of light pastry containing cheese and was often mentioned from around 1440 onward. Over the years, however, the cheese disappeared from the recipe, and lemon or orange and almonds were substituted. But the word "chess," a housewifely corruption of "cheese," has remained in the name to this day.

PASTRY CRUST MIX *for 12 tart shells (page 131)*
1¾ *cups sugar*

6 to 8 tablespoons lemon juice
rind of 2 lemons, grated
½ cup butter

Prepare and bake 12 tart shells.

Mix sugar, juice, and rind.

Melt butter in top of double boiler. Add sugar mixture and eggs.

Continue cooking over hot water until very thick, stirring constantly.

Cool, cover, and refrigerate.

When chilled, fill tart shells.

PECAN PIE
(one 9-inch pie)

The pecan tree, native to the banks of the Illinois and Mississippi rivers, fascinated Thomas Jefferson. Many times he wrote to his friends requesting some nuts: "I shall set great value on the chance of having a grove of them." In time, he planted hundreds of pecan trees and was generous in giving nuts to his friends. On March 25, 1775, George Washington planted at Mount Vernon pecans that Jefferson had sent him. Three of the trees are still growing on the banks of the Potomac. According to tradition, some of the pecan trees at the St. George Tucker House in Williamsburg grew from pecans Jefferson gave Tucker.

PASTRY CRUST MIX *for 9-inch*
  pie (page 131)
4 eggs
¾ cup sugar
½ teaspoon salt

1½ cups light corn syrup
1 tablespoon butter, melted
1 teaspoon vanilla
1 cup pecan halves

Preheat oven to 400° F.
Prepare pie shell.
Beat eggs lightly and add sugar, salt, corn syrup, cooled butter, and vanilla; stir until mixed well.
Spread pecan halves on bottom crust and cover with the filling.
Place in oven and immediately reduce heat to 350° F.
Bake 40 to 50 minutes or until mixture is firm in center.
Cool before serving.

137

BICENTENNIAL TART
(12–14 servings)

PASTRY CRUST MIX *for 10-inch pie shell (page 131)*
1 pound dried beans
VANILLA CREAM CUSTARD *(page 139)*
SPONGECAKE *(page 139)*
3 tablespoons sugar, divided
¼ cup water
4 tablespoons kirsch
2 pints fresh strawberries, washed and hulled

2 medium bananas, sliced and brushed with lemon juice
½ pint fresh blueberries, washed and hulled, or ½ can blueberry pie filling
1 cup apricot jam, forced through a sieve
1 tablespoon brandy
½ cup almonds, sliced and toasted

Preheat oven to 375° F.

Grease a 10-inch tart pan 1½ inches deep and line with dough. Prick bottom and sides with a fork. Place greased wax paper over the dough and fill with dried beans to prevent the dough from rising.

Bake at 375° F. for 35 minutes. Remove from oven, empty the beans, remove paper, prick bottom, and return to oven for about 5 minutes or until shell is a golden brown.

Place on rack and cool.

Line bottom of cooled tart shell with Vanilla Cream Custard.

Make a sugar syrup by dissolving 2 tablespoons sugar in ¼ cup water. Bring to a boil, remove from heat, and add the kirsch.

Place the Spongecake on top of the custard, and slowly spoon the sugar syrup over the surface of the cake.

Beginning at the outside edge of the tart, put on 2 rows of strawberries, hulled ends down. Add a row of overlapping banana slices, and fill the center with blueberries.

In a small saucepan, bring the apricot jam and 1 tablespoon sugar to a boil, stirring constantly. Remove from heat and add the brandy.

Spoon the glaze over the fruit.

Paint the sides of the tart with glaze and press on the almonds.

VANILLA CREAM CUSTARD

5 egg yolks
½ cup sugar
2 tablespoons cornstarch

2 cups milk
1 teaspoon vanilla

Beat egg yolks and sugar rapidly to blend well.
In a saucepan, dissolve cornstarch in ½ cup milk. Add the rest of the milk and the vanilla and bring to a boil, stirring constantly.
Pour gradually into the egg mixture and blend well.
Return to heat and boil, stirring constantly, 2 minutes.
Cool in the refrigerator until needed.

SPONGECAKE

3 eggs, separated
⅔ cup cake flour, measured
  after sifting
½ cup sugar

1 teaspoon vanilla
pinch of cream of tartar
4 tablespoons butter, melted
  and cooled slightly

Preheat oven to 350° F.
Grease well and lightly flour bottom and sides of a 9-inch round cake pan.
Beat the egg yolks 1 minute, then gradually add the sugar and beat 4 minutes. Add vanilla.
Beat the egg whites until foamy, add the pinch of cream of tartar, and beat on high speed until they form very high peaks.
Lightly and delicately fold ¼ of the whites into the yolks mixture. Then fold in ⅓ of the flour, ¼ of the whites,⅓ of the flour, ¼ of the whites, ⅓ of the flour, and the remaining ¼ of the whites.
Add the butter, folding just enough to mix well. Pour into the prepared pan.
Bake at 350° 20 minutes or until done. Do not overbake. Cool in the pan 10 minutes, then turn out onto a rack.

Cakes and Frostings

Great-great-grandmother's cake recipes can sound appalling as well as amusing; the cakemaker of today is infinitely luckier than the cakemaker of ancestral days.

The number of eggs called for in the old recipes seems needlessly extravagant, until we recall that colonial hens, who had to scratch for their living, laid much smaller eggs than do their scientifically bred, fed, pampered, and confined successors of this century. Egg yolks and whites were then beaten with forks or hickory rods; think of the length of time it took to beat the eggs for big cakes! It was a lucky day for housewives when an egg beater was patented in 1870. Marion Harland, author of *Common Sense in the Household*, who bought her egg beater in 1871, could thereafter turn out a meringue in five minutes, she testified, and make "snow custard in less than half an hour with no tremulousness of nerve or tendon."

Sugar, imported from the West Indies in colonial times, was costly and came in large, cone-shaped loaves, which had to be broken down. Among the cakes then popular was the "black cake that will last a year," if properly stored—the forerunner of the Christmas cakes and puddings of today.

140

The Raleigh Tavern Bakery is a scene of ▶ *aromatic activity as one of the bakers rakes the fire out of an oven while another waits to put in a pan of gingerbread cookies. In the foreground, Sally Lunn, Indian Corn Sticks and Muffins.*

LAYER CAKE

(three 9-inch layers)

1½ cups butter
2 cups sugar
4 eggs
3 cups sifted all-purpose flour

3 teaspoons baking powder
1 teaspoon salt
1 cup milk
1 teaspoon vanilla

Preheat oven to 350° F.

Grease three 9-inch cake pans and dust lightly with flour.

Cream butter and sugar.

Add one egg at a time, beating well after each addition.

Sift dry ingredients together and add alternately with milk and vanilla.

Pour into prepared pans and bake at 350° F. for 20 to 25 minutes.

Cool and frost with Caramel Frosting (page 149); Chocolate Frosting (page 150); Sea Foam Frosting (page 150); Seven-Minute Frosting (page 151); or Sherry Frosting (page 151).

LAYER CAKE

(two 9-inch layers)

1 cup butter
1⅓ cups sugar
2 eggs
2½ cups sifted all-purpose flour

2½ teaspoons baking powder
¾ teaspoon salt
¾ cup milk
1 teaspoon vanilla

Follow instructions for three-layer cake (*above*), but use two 9-inch pans.

◄ *Home-made ice cream served with Williamsburg Inn Pecan Bars is a popular choice for dessert on the shady terrace of the Williamsburg Inn on a summer afternoon. Shown here are: Orange Sherbet, Pepper- mint Stick Ice Cream, Rum Raisin Ice Cream, Chowning's Tavern Black Walnut Ice Cream, Vanilla Ice Cream, Lemon Ice, Raspberry Ice, and King's Arms Tavern Greengage Plum Ice Cream.*

WILLIAMSBURG LODGE
ORANGE WINE CAKE

½ cup butter
½ cup shortening
1½ cups sugar
4 eggs
1½ cups buttermilk
3½ cups sifted cake flour,
  divided
2 teaspoons baking soda

½ teaspoon salt
2 teaspoons orange extract
1 tablespoon orange rind,
  grated
1 cup raisins, finely chopped
1 cup pecans, finely chopped
SHERRY FROSTING *(page 151)*

Preheat oven to 350° F.

Lightly grease and flour two 9-inch round or three 8-inch round cake pans.

Cream butter, shortening, and sugar.

Gradually beat in the eggs and buttermilk alternately with the sifted dry ingredients. Add the orange extract and orange rind.

Scrape down the bowl occasionally and blend until smooth.

Dredge chopped raisins in ¼ cup of flour. Add raisins and pecans to the mixture.

Divide batter into prepared pans.

Bake at 350° F. for 30 minutes for 9-inch layers and 35 minutes for 8-inch layers, or until cake tests done.

Remove from oven and cool 5 minutes in pans. Turn out on cooling racks and finish cooling.

Frost with Sherry Frosting.

BANANA CAKE

2 cups sifted all-purpose flour
1 teaspoon baking powder
1 teaspoon baking soda
¾ teaspoon salt
1⅓ cups sugar
½ cup shortening

½ cup milk
1 cup ripe bananas, mashed
½ cup buttermilk
2 eggs
½ cup nuts, chopped

Preheat oven to 350° F.

Grease and flour a 10 x 5 x 3-inch pan.

Sift the dry ingredients into a mixing bowl and add the shortening, milk, bananas, and buttermilk. Beat 2 minutes on low to medium speed of an electric mixer, scraping bowl as needed.

Add eggs and beat 1 minute more.

Stir in nuts.

Pour into prepared cake pan and bake for 45 to 50 minutes at 350° F. or until cake tests done when pressed lightly in the center.

Cool in pan 10 minutes before turning out on rack.

BOURBON PECAN CAKE

2 teaspoons nutmeg, freshly grated
½ cup bourbon
1½ cups sifted all-purpose flour, divided
2 cups pecans, finely chopped
1 cup seedless raisins, finely chopped

½ cup butter
1 cup plus 2 tablespoons sugar
3 eggs, separated
1 teaspoon baking powder
dash salt
pecan halves
maraschino cherries

Preheat oven to 325° F.

Line the bottom of a 10-inch tube cake pan with brown paper and grease.

Soak nutmeg in bourbon.

Mix ½ cup flour with the nuts and raisins, coating thoroughly. Reserve.

Cream butter and sugar until light and fluffy.

Add egg yolks, one at a time, beating well after each addition.

Beat in remaining flour, baking powder, and salt.

Beat in bourbon-nutmeg mixture and continue beating until batter is well mixed.

Add the floured nuts and raisins and mix well so that they are evenly distributed in the batter.

Beat the egg whites until very stiff. Fold in.

Spoon batter into prepared pan. Press down firmly to squeeze out air pockets and allow to stand 10 minutes.

Bake at 325° F. for 1¼ hours or until cake tests done.

Cool in the pan, right side up, 1 to 2 hours before turning out. Continue cooling.

Decorate the top with pecan halves and drained maraschino cherries.

Note: This cake improves with age. Wrap it in a napkin that has been soaked in bourbon and store in a covered container for several days.

DEVIL'S FOOD CAKE

1½ cups milk, divided
4 ounces unsweetened chocolate
1½ cups sugar, divided
½ cup butter

1 teaspoon vanilla
2 eggs
¾ teaspoon salt
2 cups sifted all-purpose flour
1 teaspoon baking soda

Preheat oven to 350° F.

Line bottoms of two 9-inch cake pans with waxed or brown paper. Grease and flour pans.

Heat 1 cup milk, chocolate, and ½ cup sugar in top of double boiler or heavy saucepan, stirring constantly until smooth; cool.

Cream butter and remaining sugar in large bowl of electric mixer.

Add vanilla and eggs and beat well.

Beat in cooled chocolate mixture.

Sift salt with flour and add alternately with remaining milk, then beat 2 minutes at medium speed before adding baking soda dissolved in 3 tablespoons boiling water.

Beat 1 minute longer.

Pour into prepared pans.

Bake at 350° F. for 25 to 30 minutes or until cake tests done.

Cool cakes in pans 10 minutes; remove from pans and finish cooling on racks.

144

Frost with Caramel Frosting (page 149), Chocolate Frosting (page 150), or Seven-Minute Frosting (page 151).

BLACK FOREST CAKE

(12–14 servings)

FUDGE CAKE *(page 146)*
1 can (17 ounces) pitted dark
   sweet cherries
2 tablespoons cornstarch
3 cups whipping cream
½ cup confectioner's sugar

⅓ cup kirsch, divided
2 cups CHOCOLATE BUTTER
   CREAM FROSTING *(page 146)*
semi-sweet bar chocolate,
   shaved or grated
maraschino cherries, stemmed

Preheat oven to 325° F.

Bake the cake in three 9-inch layers at 325° F. for 30 to 35 minutes, or until cake tests done. Cool 10 minutes in pans, then turn out on racks to finish cooling.

Drain liquid from cherries into small saucepan; reserve cherries.

Bring liquid to a boil. Mix cornstarch with ¼ cup water, and stir into juice. Cook until clear.

Add cherries; cool.

Whip cream until soft peaks form. Sprinkle sugar over cream and continue beating until firm peaks form on beater when lifted from bowl.

Pour in ¼ cup kirsch a little at a time, beating only until it is taken up by the cream.

Place one layer of cake on large cake plate.

Use plain ½-inch tube or plain nozzle of cookie press to form 3 rings of Chocolate Butter Cream Frosting on bottom layer, leaving about 1½-inches between rings. Chill.

Fill in between rings with cherries.

Place second layer gently on top of cherries.

Prick top all over with fork, sprinkle lightly with kirsch, and spread it with 1 inch of whipped cream.

Put top layer on gently. Spread sides and top with remaining whipped cream.

Garnish top with chocolate curls, a whipped cream rosette or dollop of whipped cream and maraschino cherries, rinsed and drained.

Refrigerate until serving time.

CHOCOLATE BUTTER CREAM FROSTING

(2 cups)

8 tablespoons butter
4 cups sifted confectioner's
  sugar
2 large egg whites or 4 small
  egg whites, unbeaten

1 teaspoon vanilla
3 ounces semi-sweet chocolate,
  melted

Cream butter, add sugar, egg whites, and vanilla.
Add chocolate and continue beating until smooth.

FUDGE CAKE

1 cup butter
2 cups sugar
4 eggs
2 cups sifted all-purpose flour
¼ teaspoon salt

1½ teaspoons baking soda
⅔ cup buttermilk
1 teaspoon vanilla
3 ounces unsweetened
  chocolate, grated

Preheat oven to 325° F.
Grease and flour a 9 x 13 x 1½-inch pan.
Cream butter and sugar.
Add eggs one at a time and beat well after each addition.
After last egg is added, beat 1 minute or until mixture is light and fluffy.
Sift flour with salt.
Mix baking soda with the buttermilk and add alternately with flour to the creamed mixture.
Add vanilla.

Melt the chocolate in ⅔ cup boiling water, stir until smooth.
Blend chocolate into cake mixture.

Pour into prepared pan and bake for 1 hour at 325° F. or until cake tests done.

Cool in pan.

Frost while slightly warm with Chocolate Frosting (page 150).

ORANGE BLOSSOMS

(6 dozen)

3 eggs
1½ cups sugar
1 teaspoon vanilla
1½ cups sifted all-purpose flour

1½ teaspoons baking powder
½ teaspoon salt
ORANGE SYRUP (*below*)

Preheat oven to 400° F.

Beat eggs until very light. Add sugar gradually, beating until light and fluffy.

Add ½ cup cold water and vanilla. Fold in sifted dry ingredients.

Rinse muffin tins (1¾ inches in diameter) in cold water but do not grease.

Bake at 400° F. about 15 minutes or until golden.

Cool 5 minutes, remove from pans, and dip into Orange Syrup.

Drain on rack.

ORANGE SYRUP

1¼ cups granulated sugar
½ cup orange juice

3 tablespoons lemon juice

Combine ingredients and bring to a boil.

Cool and refrigerate 24 hours before using.

SPICY CARROT CAKE

1½ cups vegetable oil
2½ cups sugar
4 eggs, separated
2½ cups sifted all-purpose flour
1½ teaspoons baking powder
½ teaspoon baking soda
¼ teaspoon salt

½ teaspoon nutmeg
1 teaspoon cinnamon
1 teaspoon ground cloves
1¾ cups raw carrots, grated,
   divided
1 cup pecans, chopped
GLAZE (*below*)

Preheat oven to 350° F.

Grease and flour 10-inch tube cake pan.

Mix oil and sugar together. Beat in egg yolks one at a time. Continue to beat and add 5 tablespoons of hot water.

Sift together flour, baking powder, baking soda, salt, and spices. Add to egg mixture.

Reserve ¼ cup grated carrots for garnish and stir in remaining carrots and pecans.

Fold in beaten egg whites.

Pour batter into prepared pan and bake at 350° F. for 60 to 70 minutes or until cake tests done.

Cool in pan right side up for 15 minutes, then turn out to finish cooling on cake rack.

Drizzle Glaze in a circle on top of cake and sprinkle with reserved grated carrot.

GLAZE

¾ cup sifted confectioner's
   sugar

3 tablespoons lemon juice

Mix above ingredients together to make glaze.

POUND CAKE

1 cup butter
1 cup sugar
6 eggs
2 cups sifted all-purpose flour

½ teaspoon baking powder
1 teaspoon orange flavoring
1 teaspoon lemon flavoring

Have all ingredients at room temperature.

148

Preheat oven to 325° F.

Grease and dust with flour a 9¼ x 5¼ x 2¾-inch loaf pan or a 9-inch tube pan.

Cream butter, gradually add sugar. Add eggs one at a time, beating well after each addition.

Sift flour and baking powder together and gradually stir into egg mixture.

Add orange and lemon flavorings.

Spoon into prepared pan.

Bake at 325° F. for 70 minutes if loaf pan is used and 60 minutes for tube pan.

WILLIAMSBURG INN
DATE NUT POUND CAKE

⅓ *cup chopped pecans* or   ⅓ *cup chopped dates*
walnuts

Follow recipe for Pound Cake (page 148), except reserve 2 tablespoons of the flour to dredge dates.

After adding dry ingredients to egg mixture, stir in pecans or walnuts and dates.

CARAMEL FROSTING

(for 2-layer cake)

¼ *cup butter*   2½ *to 3 cups sifted*
¾ *cup light brown sugar,*   *confectioner's sugar*
packed   1 *teaspoon vanilla*
¼ *cup evaporated milk*   *dash of salt*

Melt butter in saucepan over medium heat and add brown sugar and milk. Heat until sugar dissolves.

Cool slightly, then beat in confectioner's sugar, vanilla, and salt.

Double the recipe to frost a 3-layer cake.

Use with Layer Cake (page 141) or Devil's Food Cake (page 144).

CHOCOLATE FROSTING

(for 2-layer cake)

*4 ounces unsweetened
  chocolate
½ cup butter
1 pound sifted confectioner's
  sugar*

*dash of salt
1 teaspoon vanilla
½ to ⅔ cup evaporated milk*

Melt chocolate and butter over hot water.

Sift sugar and salt together and add the vanilla and choco-late mixture.

Add enough milk to make spreading consistency.

Increase ingredients by ½ to frost a 3-layer cake.

Use with Layer Cake (page 141), Devil's Food Cake (page 144), or Fudge Cake (page 146).

SEA FOAM FROSTING

(for 2-layer cake)

*1½ cups light brown sugar,
  packed
¼ teaspoon cream of tartar*

*dash of salt
2 egg whites
1 teaspoon vanilla*

Combine sugar, cream of tartar, and salt in ½ cup water and stir over low heat until sugar is dissolved.

Bring mixture to a boil, stirring and cooking until mixture spins a thread (264° F. on a candy thermometer).

Pour over beaten egg whites, beating constantly. Do not scrape the pan but allow cooked mixture to run out.

Add vanilla and continue beating until of spreading consist-ency.

Double the recipe to frost a 3-layer cake.

Use with Layer Cake (page 141).

150

SEVEN-MINUTE FROSTING

(for 2-layer cake)

2 egg whites
1 tablespoon light corn syrup
　or ¼ teaspoon cream of tartar

1½ cups sugar
1 teaspoon vanilla

Combine all ingredients except vanilla in ⅓ cup water in the top of a double boiler.

Beat until well blended, about 1 minute on high speed of electric beater.

Place over rapidly boiling water and beat constantly for 5 to 8 minutes, or until mixture forms soft peaks.

Remove from water and add vanilla. Turn frosting into a bowl and continue to beat for 2 minutes.

Double the recipe to frost a 3-layer cake.

Use with Layer Cake(page 141)or Devil's Food Cake (page 144).

SHERRY FROSTING

(for 2-layer cake)

¼ cup butter
2½ to 3 cups sifted
　confectioner's sugar
¼ cup orange juice

½ teaspoon orange flavoring
dash salt
½ teaspoon orange rind, grated
dry sherry

Cream butter and add remaining ingredients except sherry.

Add enough sherry, approximately 1 tablespoon, to make frosting of spreading consistency. If frosting is too thin, add more sugar or refrigerate it.

Double the recipe to frost a 3-layer cake.

Use with Layer Cake (page 141), or Williamsburg Lodge Orange Wine Cake (page 142).

Cookies

BOURBON BALLS

(36–42 balls)

2 cups vanilla wafer crumbs
2 tablespoons cocoa
1½ cups confectioner's sugar,
  divided

1 cup pecans, very finely
  chopped
2 tablespoons white corn syrup
¼ cup bourbon

Mix well vanilla wafer crumbs, cocoa, 1 cup confectioner's sugar, and pecans.

Add corn syrup and bourbon; mix well.

Shape into 1-inch balls and roll in remaining confectioner's sugar.

Put in tightly covered tin box or other metal container for at least 12 hours before serving.

Note: These cookies keep well for 4 or 5 weeks.

RUM BALLS

(36–42 balls)

Follow recipe for Bourbon Balls (*above*).
Substitute ¼ cup rum for the bourbon.

BRANDY BALLS

(36–42 balls)

Follow recipe for Bourbon Balls (*above*).
Substitute ¼ cup brandy for the bourbon.

CINNAMON SQUARES

(48 squares)

½ cup butter
½ cup margarine
1 cup sugar
1 egg, separated

2 cups sifted all-purpose flour
1½ tablespoons cinnamon
1 teaspoon salt
1½ cups nuts, chopped

Preheat oven to 325° F.

Grease and flour a 16 x 11 x 1-inch pan.

Cream butter, margarine, and sugar. Add egg yolk and sifted dry ingredients.

Press batter into prepared pan.

Beat egg white until foamy and spread sparingly over batter (not all the egg white will be used).

Press on nuts.

Bake at 325° F. for 30 minutes.

Cut into squares.

COFFEE CRISPS

(36 cookies)

⅓ cup butter
⅓ cup margarine
½ cup light brown sugar,
  packed
1 egg, beaten lightly
1 teaspoon rum extract

2 cups sifted all-purpose flour
⅛ teaspoon baking soda
½ teaspoon baking powder
½ teaspoon salt
2 tablespoons instant coffee
pecans, chopped or halves

Preheat oven to 400° F. 10 minutes before cookies are to be put in.

Grease cookie sheet.

Cream butter, margarine, and sugar.

Add the egg and rum extract and mix well.

Beat in sifted dry ingredients.

Shape dough into rolls 2 inches in diameter, wrap in waxed paper, and chill.

154

When firm, cut into thin slices and top with nuts.
Bake on prepared cookie sheet at 400° F. for 12 to 15 minutes.

HOLIDAY COOKIES

(36 cookies)

½ cup butter, softened   2 cups sifted all-purpose flour
1 cup sugar   1½ teaspoons baking powder
1 egg, beaten   ½ teaspoon salt
1 teaspoon vanilla   colored sugar
1 tablespoon whipping cream

Preheat oven to 375° F. 10 minutes before cookies are to be put in.

Grease cookie sheet.

Cream butter and sugar. Add egg, vanilla, cream and sifted dry ingredients.

Chill in refrigerator several hours.

Roll out, cut, and sprinkle with colored sugar.

Place at least 3 inches apart on prepared cookie sheet (they spread quite a bit).

Bake at 375° F. for 15 minutes.

Note: If not served immediately, store in covered container to retain crispness.

ORANGE NUT BARS

(21–28 bars)

3 eggs   ¼ teaspoon salt
1 can (6 ounces) frozen orange   1 cup chopped nuts
  juice concentrate   1 package (8 ounces) pitted
1 cup sugar   dates, chopped
2 cups graham cracker crumbs   1 teaspoon vanilla
1 teaspoon baking powder   ORANGE ICING *(page 156)*

Preheat oven to 350° F.

Grease and lightly flour a 9-inch-square pan.

Beat eggs until light and fluffy. Beat in orange juice concentrate. Stir in remaining ingredients and mix well.

Spoon mixture into prepared pan.

Bake at 350° F. for 50 minutes.

Remove from oven and cool in pan on rack.

Frost with Orange Icing and cut into bars.

ORANGE ICING

1¼ cups confectioner's sugar   2½ tablespoons orange juice

Beat until smooth and spread.

WILLIAMSBURG INN
PECAN BARS

(54 bars)

1 cup butter
1 cup light brown sugar,
  packed
1 cup honey

¼ cup whipping cream
3 cups pecans, chopped
SUGAR DOUGH *(page 157)*,
  partially baked

Preheat oven to 350° F.

Put butter, sugar, and honey in deep, heavy-bottomed saucepan; stir and boil 5 minutes. Remove from heat.

Cool slightly and add cream and chopped pecans; mix well.

Spread topping evenly over surface of the partially baked Sugar Dough with a buttered wooden spoon or flexible spatula.

Bake for 30 to 35 minutes at 350° F.

Cool and cut into 1 x 2-inch bars.

In the soft glow of candlelight, the dining room of the George Wythe House is set once again with tempting eighteenth-century desserts—three Pound Cakes baked in Turk's-head molds, Ambrosia (center), Pecan Pie, Apple Dumplings, and Wine Jelly Molds, with marzipan filling the top glass. Sweetmeats and fruit are arranged on the creamware épergne.

SUGAR DOUGH

¾ cup butter
¾ cup sugar
2 eggs

rind of 1 lemon, grated
3 cups sifted all-purpose flour
½ teaspoon baking powder
PECAN TOPPING *(page 156.)*

Preheat oven to 375° F. 10 minutes before dough is ready to go into oven.

Grease and flour two 9 x 9 x 2-inch baking pans.

Cream butter and sugar; add eggs and lemon rind and beat well.

Sift flour and baking powder together, add to creamed mixture, and beat well.

Chill dough until firm enough to handle.

Press dough onto bottom and sides of prepared pans. Dough will be approximately ⅛-inch thick. Prick all over with a fork.

Bake 12 to 15 minutes at 375° F. or until dough looks half done.

Remove from oven and spread with Pecan Topping *(page 156)*.

◄ *The Raleigh Tavern bar, where many a colonial gentleman quenched his thirst, is the background for a variety of typical Williamsburg beverages. Left to right: Chowning's Tavern Wine Cooler, Eggnog, Champagne Punch, Wine Punch, Fish House Punch, and Sherry.*

Beverages

Alcoholic beverages were a household staple in colonial Virginia. There were no aspirins, no tranquilizers, and no anesthetics, so brandy or rum often was used in their stead. Too, a good drink was regarded as a preventive against flux and fever, which is why many an early-rising planter fortified himself with a starter before making the rounds of his plantation.

Rare was the Virginia gentleman, however, who failed to conduct himself with "great Decency and good Order," drinks or no drinks. Gentlemen had to set an example. Else how could they hope to keep the field hands and servants sober? "The parson and I returned to our quarters in good time and good order," wrote William Byrd on March 2, 1728, "but my man Tom broke the rules of hospitality by getting extremely drunk in a civil house." It was a problem.

Thomas Jefferson was an acknowledged connoisseur of foreign wines. He supported a proposed reduction of duties on wine to avoid the use of whisky as a substitute. Wine he declared to be a necessity of life and said no nation is drunk where wine is cheap.

Claret was Washington's favorite wine. When the Marquis de Chastellux presented him with a cask, Washington replied, "You can relieve me by promising to partake very often of that hilarity which a Glass of good Claret seldom fails to produce."

CHOWNING'S TAVERN
WINE COOLER

(1 serving)

¾ *glass lemonade*   *sprig of mint*
¼ *glass claret*   *maraschino cherry*

This makes a colorful as well as refreshing drink if the liquids are not mixed together. Pour the lemonade over crushed ice, then the claret.

Garnish with a sprig of mint and a cherry.

Good for hot days.

PUNCH

Although much was said in praise of wine, more was said of punch. This was the Tidewater's standby drink. "Punch" is the English rendering of the Hindustani *pauch*, meaning five, for the five ingredients—spirits, water, sliced lemons or limes, sugar, and spice.

Ned Ward, an eighteenth-century English tavern-keeper and satirist, intoxicated by the merits of this concoction, penned the following couplet in its praise:

> Immortal Drink, whose compound is of Five,
> More praise dost thou deserve than man can give.

The recipe for the immortal drink came to England from the Far East, together with tea, root ginger, and spice, fine East Indian muslins and cashmere shawls, and other new delights, either by way of the fourteenth-century caravan route or by sea around the Cape of Good Hope.

In the Tidewater, rum from the West Indies and brandy were the chief ingredients of punch. In December, 1710, William Byrd II described the afternoon's activity: "My wife and I made some punch of [lemons] white sack, and Madeira brandy, and I put it into bottles."

A bowl of punch was the planters' most companionable drink. Many a political strategy was hatched, many a long evening of pleasure was spent with a small punch bowl at each right elbow. The punch made by one of Williamsburg's tavern-keepers, Henry Wetherburn, figures in a story that is still remembered today. In May 1736, after planter William Randolph agreed to sell some of his farm land to Thomas Jefferson's father, he insisted on Henry Wetherburn's "biggest bowl of Arrack punch" to seal the bargain.

WINE PUNCH

(12 servings)

1 bottle red wine	2 lemons, sliced
1 cup orange juice	3 oranges, sliced
1 cup pineapple juice	

Combine all of the ingredients and pour over a block of ice.

CHAMPAGNE PUNCH

(15 servings)

1 bottle champagne, chilled	½ bottle sparkling water,
½ cup brandy	chilled
½ cup Cointreau	

Combine all of the ingredients and serve in punch cups.

FISH HOUSE PUNCH

(10–15 servings)

1 cup light brown sugar, packed	1 fifth dark rum
9 lemons	½ fifth cognac
2 cups pineapple juice	4 tablespoons peach brandy

Mix sugar and 4 cups water in a pan and boil 5 minutes.

Squeeze the juice from the lemons and pour into the hot syrup. Add the lemon rinds.

Cool syrup and refrigerate overnight.

Just before serving, remove the lemon rinds. Add the pine-apple juice and liquors.

Pack a large punch bowl with crushed ice. Pour the punch over the ice and serve.

HOT SPICED PUNCH

(8 servings)

1 quart apple cider　　　　　*1 teaspoon nutmeg*
3 cinnamon sticks　　　　　　*1 teaspoon whole cloves*
4 tablespoons lemon juice

Simmer cider, cinnamon sticks, and lemon juice for 15 minutes.

Tie nutmeg and cloves in a small cheesecloth bag and put into simmering cider long enough to give it the desired taste.

WASSAIL

(20 servings)

Wassailing is an ancient English custom, part of the feasts and revelry of New Year's Eve and New Year's Day, which has been revived in Colonial Williamsburg. The master of the English household drank the health of those present with a bowl of spiced ale, and each in turn after him passed the bowl along and repeated the Saxon phrase *Wass hael,* "be whole," or "be well."

1 cup sugar　　　　　　*2 cups orange juice*
4 cinnamon sticks　　　*6 cups claret*
lemon slices　　　　　　*½ cup lemon juice*
2 cups pineapple juice　*1 cup dry sherry*

Boil sugar, cinnamon sticks, and 3 lemon slices in ½ cup water for 5 minutes and strain.

Heat but do not boil the remaining ingredients.

Combine with syrup, garnish with lemon slices, and serve hot.

EGGNOG

(*40 servings*)

The drink called eggnog in America may be an adaptation of milk punch, an old English drink made with milk, eggs, brandy, sugar, and lemon juice. In February 1796, Isaac Weld wrote that he and several other travelers who had stopped in Philadelphia at the same house all breakfasted together: "The American travellers, before they pursued their journey, took a hearty draught each, according to custom, of egg-nog, a mixture composed of new milk, eggs, rum, and sugar, beat up together."

12 eggs, separated　　*½ teaspoon salt*
1 cup sugar　　　　　*3 pints whipping cream*
1 cup bourbon　　　　*nutmeg*
1 cup cognac

Beat egg yolks with sugar until thick.
Slowly add bourbon and cognac.
Chill several hours.

162

Whip egg whites with salt until stiff.
Whip cream and add both to egg yolk mixture.
Chill 1 hour.
Sprinkle with nutmeg.
Note: For thinner eggnog pour 1 cup of milk in with egg yolks.

Index

Entries in *italics* refer to illustrations on facing page unless otherwise noted

Index

Index

170

Index